The New
Manager's
Guide to
Success

The New Manager's Guide to Success

James R. Baehler

PRAEGER

PRAEGER SPECIAL STUDIES • PRAEGER SCIENTIFIC

Library of Congress Cataloging in Publication Data

Baehler, James R
   The new manager's guide to success.

   1. Management. I. Title.
HD31.B314   658.4   80-19509
ISBN 0-03-058014-5

Published in 1980 by Praeger Publishers
CBS Educational and Professional Publishing
A Division of CBS, Inc.
521 Fifth Avenue, New York, New York 10017 U.S.A.

© 1980 by Praeger Publishers

0123456789   145   987654321

Printed in the United States of America

FOREWORD

The transition to management is one of the most difficult steps in your entire career. You earned your promotion by performing your job well, but now your performance depends upon other people, and they are probably not as talented and motivated as you are.

You developed a set of skills through training and experience; you were a good engineer, clerk, or sales representative. But these skills will not help you to perform as a manager. In fact, continuing to think and act as an engineer, clerk, or sales representative can actually harm your managerial performance.

You must now think about yourself and other people in a fundamentally new way. You are a manager, a member of the management team. Instead of doing things yourself, you must learn how to get other people to do them. Instead of regarding management as *them*, you must regard management as *us*. Instead of complaining about policies, you must support and implement them.

To make this difficult transition you will need a great deal of help. If you are lucky, your boss and associates will provide guidance and coaching, but don't be surprised if they don't do it. They have their own problems and may not be willing to help with yours. Even if they want to help, they may not have the time or knowledge to provide useful guidance on the entire range of managerial tasks and problems.

This book can provide some of the help you need, and it can guide you to other useful sources. It covers all the critical issues a new manager faces: hiring people, analyzing jobs, appraising performance, communicating orally and in writing, even dressing properly. And it discusses them in clear, simple English. Instead of trying to impress you with footnotes and jargon, it directly tells you what to do and how to do it.

I suggest that you read the book as soon as possible, then keep it handy. When you have a communications problem, or must fire someone, or do not know how to analyze a problem, pick it up and refer to the appropriate chapter. I'm sure that you will find it helpful.

Alan Schoonmaker, Ph.D.
Management Consultant

CONTENTS

INTRODUCTION

As a new manager in business you have just taken an important step in the effort to succeed in your new job. You recognize that there are skills and understandings that you do not have and so have bought this book to help overcome those shortcomings. A recognition of a deficiency must precede the effort to correct it. You have acknowledged that there are things you need to learn about functioning successfully as a manager and you have done something about it. If you continue this questioning approach to your knowledge and skills your success as a manager is almost assured.

Much of what you need to know as a manager can be found in books and periodicals. If you haven't yet discovered Peter Drucker, it is time to do so. His books and articles on management deal not just with theory but, more important, with its application. Although much of Drucker's writing is aimed at senior managers, a great deal of it is immediately pertinent to first-line managers who can benefit from insight into the problems of senior management. Someday you may be facing similar problems, and in management, as in most areas of life, early preparation is always beneficial.

Another valuable source of management information is the *Harvard Business Review*. Published six times a year, it consistently contains the most thought-provoking and useful articles in the business world. In addition to publishing current business writing, the *Review* offers a reprint service for past articles. The best start is to order the package of their fifteen best selling reprints. These articles have become classics of business writing and cover such topics as communication, performance appraisal, problem analysis, and leadership, as well as other relevant subjects.

Aside from written material much valuable information can be obtained from more experienced managers, with whom you should not hesitate to discuss your problems. Your immediate boss has a vested interest in your success and should be a valuable resource. Other managers can provide a diversity of experiences and viewpoints that will be equally helpful. On a note of caution, however, it is sometimes best to consult with managers who are outside your company. Aside from with your boss, be cautious about discussing your department's problems within your company. Such discussions should only be held with persons whom you trust completely and who will not use your problems to advance their own careers. Competition in business is necessary and useful but sometimes its spirit can be perverted by individuals who are unscrupulous in their efforts to advance. Your boss should be kept fully aware of any problems in your department but it is seldom necessary to involve other people in the company. It is to your advantage to have two or three experienced business people from outside your company to whom you can turn for advice and counsel. Such mentors prove a valuable adjunct to almost every successful career in business.

This book is designed to assist you in functioning effectively as a manager. It is arranged so that basic management theories are presented simply and then related to practical situations. Wherever possible you will be given the opportunity to apply management theories to the problems of your job or to self-analysis. Every attempt has been made to make the information practical and useful. Business literature is filled with theories and abstract discussions but there is a dearth of information about what to do as a manager. Wherever possible at the end of a chapter you will be given something to do that will help you function more effectively as a manager. The underlying assumption of this book is that management is a competency that can be learned.

Effective management is the application of skills so that a desired result is attained; it is not a mental exercise. A manager must act, not just think. Thought without action accomplishes nothing, but action without thought can easily produce negative results. The accomplishment of a task almost always involves securing the efficient efforts of other people and this requires an understanding and application of management skills.

To acquire the skills of management, you must follow a specific course of action:

- Determine what skills are required.

- Determine to what extent you already possess those skills.

- Develop a program for skill improvement.

- Practice the application of your skills.
- Objectively analyze the results of skill application.
- Modify behavior based upon analysis of results.

This book will outline the basic managerial skills you will need, it will help you examine yourself to determine your present skill level, and it will assist in the development of an action plan for improvement. Beyond that you must consciously practice your skills, analyze the results, and alter your behavior to produce better results. This is the one sure path to success as a manager. A sure path to failure is to assume that improvement will come automatically as you spend time in your job. Improvement is not an incidental by-product of job tenure, it is the result of conscious directed effort.

This book is intended to be used, not read through and then set aside. There are some chapters (Job Analysis, Motivation, Leadership) that every manager immediately will need to read and begin to apply. Other chapters (Performance Appraisal, Hiring) may have a practical application at a later time. The book will serve as a reference work so that a manager faced with a particular problem can refer to the appropriate chapter and receive guidance on effective behavior.

Good luck, and now on to Chapter 1 and the first step on your road to success as a manager in American business.

The New
Manager's
Guide to
Success

1THE GAME OF BUSINESS

Y ou are a player in the most exciting and rewarding game that has ever been devised, the game of business. It is played in every country of the world by men and women of all ages and abilities. Those who reach the highest levels in the business game achieve wealth and status that far exceeds the dreams they had when they first began the game. They also have the satisfaction of knowing that their efforts have provided jobs and earnings for a multitude of others.

The best part of the business game is that it can be played by almost anyone. It does not require extraordinary physical skill or intellectual ability. Success in business comes to the able, the dedicated, the persistent, the risk-taker, and the fortunate. All these characteristics, except the last, can be developed by anyone with just average inherent abilities, and as to the last, Tertullian noted that "Fortune favors the brave." Those who succeed in business are seldom the brightest or most congenial; the game is won by those who make the most of their abilities and who can focus on the few things that lead to success.

One of the most interesting and disconcerting aspects of the game of business is that its rules are not written down for all to see and follow. Because the game is subtle, players must discover the rules for themselves. Those who are unable to do so remain lost in the minor leagues of business. Occasionally one who seems to break the rules will rise to the top but, in general, those who succeed learn the rules early and how to use them to best advantage.

Let us look at some of the basic rules of business.

- Set both short- and long-term goals for yourself. These goals do not refer to your job but to your career. Where do you want to be five years from now? Ten? Fifteen?

- Plot your career path. Once your long-term goals are established, decide what is necessary to achieve them. What additional skills, knowledge, and experience will you need? What are the interim jobs you should hold to reach your goal?

- Set a time line. You should not spend more than three to four years in any one job because by then you will have learned 80 percent to 90 percent of what can be learned. From then on your learning curve drops off so sharply that you will just be marking time.

- Change jobs. Do not be categorized as "manufacturing" or "marketing" or any other single element. Get to know all aspects of the business, especially finance. If necessary, change companies to gain wider experience.

- Reveal only your next step or your short-term goals. You are liable to be frowned upon if you reveal your ambition to be president of the company.

- Probably the most useful thing you can do to improve your chances for promotion is to let your superiors know that you are ambitious. Ask them what it will take for you to move up to the next rung on the ladder.

- Learn the language of business, especially financial terms. As you move up in the managerial ranks, financial understanding becomes increasingly important. If finance is alien to you take introductory courses in managerial finance and accounting at your local college.

- Line positions are best. Marketing and sales are where the action is. Everything else in the company—finance, manufacturing, data processing, and personnel—really exists only to serve the sales department. Your career path should include some time in sales or marketing.

- Make things happen. Planners are necessary but they usually report to doers. Know what is expected of you and make sure it happens on schedule.

- Never promise more than you can deliver. If you do, you violate the next rule.

- Make your boss look good.

- Be competitive. People who want to win in the business game make certain they do win: You must feel that you control events and that your efforts can produce the desired outcomes.

- Look at your job from above. How does the president of the company view the work of your unit? How does it fit in with the work of other units? Do not see yourself in isolation. You are part of a big picture so keep that big picture in focus and devise ways in which your unit can be of greater help to other units.

- Create an image of competence. Speak purposefully and concisely. Know the facts and objectively analyze them to draw your conclusions. Walk and move briskly. Express decisions confidently.

- Protect your status and your turf.

- Dress one level up.

These are the basic rules of the game of business. The remainder of this book is aimed at helping you apply some of those rules.

2 WOMEN IN BUSINESS

*Where the willingness is great, the
difficulty cannot be great.*

*There is nothing more difficult to
take in hand, more perilous to
conduct or more uncertain in its
success, than to take the lead in a
new order of things.*—Machiavelli

Business was designed by men to be practiced by men for the
benefit of men. The rules, customs, and techniques of business
are an outgrowth of an apparently universal male urge to compete.
For hundreds of years men assumed that the competitive urge was
uniquely theirs and that the occasional woman who entered business was an odd creature untypical of her sex. It was only grudg-
ingly that men allowed women to enter business and then only as
serving maidens to the dominant males. In fact, it was not until the
typewriter began to generate copious quantities of business documents that women in any significant numbers began to enter the
business world. Women were discovered to be particularly adept at
producing these documents and filing and retrieving them; they
were *in* the business world but not *of* it. They were part of the
mechanical process by which documents were produced, stored,
and retrieved, but they were not part of the intellectual process by
which plans were developed, decisions made, and activities directed.

As women in offices served their typewriters so women in
factories served their looms, sewing machines, and other equipment. Although factory women were part of the manufacturing
process, they were not involved in its control. The advantage that

WOMEN IN BUSINESS • 5

the factory owner saw in women was that, unlike machinery, they were a variable expense that could be reduced in slack times and expanded in good times.

If a businessman of the nineteenth century had been asked to foretell the future of women in business his answer probably would have reflected uncertainty as to the meaning of the question. The future of women in business would be the same as in the past—willing hands that served their machines. What else could there be? A vision of women as managers would leave Mr. Nineteenth-Century Businessman completely befuddled. Why, everyone knew that women were constitutionally incapable of participating in the management of a business enterprise. Such activity demanded foresight, prudence, firm resolve, a mastery of technical details, and a calm, reasoned approach to problems. The Good Lord in His infinite wisdom had bestowed those qualities upon men only. To women He had given gentleness, forbearance, a loving nature, and an intellect that, while charming, was dominated by emotion and illogical thought patterns. Worst of all women were not competitive; they didn't understand the importance of winning. No, I'm sorry. Women as managers? Unthinkable, absolute rubbish!

For women of today, there is both good news and bad news. The bad news is that much of that nineteenth-century attitude still exists. The good news is that it is changing, slowly but perceptibly.

Women are entering business as managers, sales people, technicians, professionals, and management trainees, not just as servants to machines. Clearly, women are not being "given" these opportunities. They exist because men were forced to make them available to women. No group in human history has ever yielded a privileged position without some force compelling them to do so.

Women did not obtain the opportunity to participate in American business because men decided that it was "right" or "morally correct" to permit them to do so. It is true that men have begun to yield their privilege of exclusive control over business, but they have done so in response to enormous pressure brought by women. As in any transfer of power, privilege is being yielded slowly with battles being fought over each advance and with much delaying action by the retreating forces.

The struggle is not over and the end is even now uncertain. It may be that women will not be able to sustain the prolonged effort necessary to achieve their goal of equality in business. If so, much but by no means all of their advances may be lost. Unless, in the years ahead, women are able to persevere they may end up as permanent middle managers of American business. Decision-making slots will be reserved for men with only an occasional woman superstar breaking into the upper atmosphere of money and power.

Unfair as this struggle may seem to women, it is as things should be. Any efficient economic system is based on competition. Every company is competing to serve its customers better. Those that do, survive and prosper; those that don't, lose their markets and die. Managers who run successful companies have learned to compete effectively. In forcing men to yield some of their privileges, women are demonstrating for the first time that they can compete. The struggle by women to secure decision making roles for themselves is the first step in the process by which women demonstrate their competency to fill those roles. Success in the struggle requires women to produce their own leaders and to simultaneously develop organizational and managerial skills. Women who achieve positions of influence because they would not permit men to deny them those positions will be respected. A worthy opponent has always been esteemed by men of character.

The situation in business today is that increasing numbers of women are found at all levels below the presidential suite. But men are still suspicious of the ability of women to function effectively as decision makers. Some of this suspicion is due to the paths that women have chosen in moving up through corporate ranks. Too many women, by choice or acquiescence, are to be found in personnel, human resources, public relations, or training departments. It is of no use, however, for women to complain that these are the only areas that men have opened to them. It may seem that men would like to restrict women to those areas because they are outside the mainstream of corporate life. All are staff functions where an unwise decision would have little or no impact on the bottom line. This is part of a basic strategy by which a battlefield is stubbornly surrendered and a delaying action is fought back to the next line of defense.

The warfare analogy cannot be carried too far because women are seeking not to annihilate their enemy but, rather, the opportunity to move into the enemy's homeland and to work there in peace with that enemy. The struggle must be conducted so that after the armistice men and women can coexist in cooperation and trust.

What does all this mean for the individual woman trying to find her own way in the world of business? What are the things she can do to advance her career? I would like to offer some observations and a few suggestions. My remarks are not addressed to those women who serve in people-related staff positions. Their niche has already been fully carved out. Their sex will be an asset since in a great many large corporations vice-presidencies of personnel, human resources, and public relations departments are reserved for women or minorities to satisfy EEO requirements. Women in those areas should make maximum use of their opportunity and use the company's need to look good on the quarterly EEO report to their own advantage.

I would like to address those women who aspire to roles as decision makers and begin by listing a few givens.

—Businessmen still have trouble perceiving women in a decision-making role.

—Businessmen are suspicious of the ability of women to master the technical details of a modern business.

—Women, with a few notable exceptions, are viewed as not being "tough" enough to manage a business.

—Men in business are apprehensive about the perceived emotionality of women.

—Men do not believe that a woman can have children and still be fully committed to a business career.

—Men feel that most women have never acquired a competitive spirit.

—Men believe that women are not sufficiently motivated by the rewards of money and status.

—Men have learned one mode of behavior when dealing with women, realize that it is inappropriate with a competent businesswoman, and are uncertain about what type of behavior is appropriate.

Obviously not every man in business shares these attitudes. They are present, however, to a greater or lesser degree, in a significant number of American businessmen. Women have remarked that this is simply a list of the problems that men have and that it is up to men to work out their own solutions, but this is a short-sighted belief. Too often a man's solution is to avoid hiring women for positions of responsibility. This solution benefits no one. It is much better for a woman to recognize that these attitudes exist and to develop an approach that will benefit both herself and the man.

In essence, the situation comes down to this: men have spent two hundred years since the birth of the Industrial Revolution learning to work together and compete against one another. They developed a game that was suited to their temperaments and satisfying to their egos. Suddenly, a different group has forced its way into the game and while men still control the game the new group is making them very uncomfortable. Unless women recognize this discomfort they are going to have difficulty in dealing with it and, perhaps, turning it to their advantage.

One consequence of this discomfort is that for a woman to advance in business she must be better than her male colleagues, not just as good. Unless a woman is clearly superior to her competition, her male boss is probably going to promote a man because he is more comfortable working with a man. To cry that this is unfair is to miss the point. Of course it's unfair but as John Kennedy used to say, "Who said that life was supposed to be fair?" Whether or not something is fair is a value judgment that interferes with an objective analysis of the situation. It is more productive for a woman to recognize the attitudes that men have, strive to change those attitudes when possible, and adjust to them when necessary. In any event, in the instance cited above if a woman is no better than her male colleagues she ought to find another field of work. The level of competence of most male middle managers is so low that anyone who cannot stand out should find another line of work.

Assuming a reasonable level of competence, what can a woman do to enhance her career?

- Go where the action is. Stay away from personnel, operations, manufacturing, and public relations. The best choices in order of preference are sales, finance, and law. Sales and finance provide the training ground for most chief executive officers. Except for capital intensive industries such as the steel industry, the major problems of American business revolve around generating sales revenue and developing financial controls to ensure profitability. If you are in the law department stay out of labor relations; try to get into an area of high visibility such as acquisitions.

- Learn the jargon of sports. Businessmen, with few exceptions, only talk about three things—business, sex, and sports. With a woman present the list is reduced to two, business and sports. Remember, you are still playing in their game and sports jargon is therefore part of the language of business. Football offers the closest corollary to business since it is also a form of warfare. Adopt the local professional or college football team as your own. Go to the games and learn the terminology and strategy. There are any number of beat-up former jocks around who will be happy to instruct you. Once you become familiar with sports terms you'll be surprised how often they can be applied to business. Instead of talking about a declining market share you can describe how "It's the fourth quarter and we're backed up to the goal line with the rain in our face."

Once you've mastered football move on to baseball. It is not analogous to business in the way that football is but almost every American male has played it, even if it was only in the schoolyard when he was a child. Instead of suggesting a change of strategy you can recommend that, ". . . we put a little spin on the ball."

Don't bother with the other sports. Hockey is a mystery to many, including the participants. No one can relate to basketball who is not eight feet tall and from either a Brooklyn slum or an Indiana farm. All soccer terms are a hybrid of German and Spanish ("Kickense La Pelota!") and cause frown wrinkles when used in America. Tennis used to be the new "in" sport but it has been replaced by racquetball, which requires little skill but great energy, ideal for American managers. Golf is played by all corporate vice-presidents but there are only two terms to be learned. "We'll play it as it lies." (Boys, we've screwed up again and we'll have to make the best of it.) "Keep your head down and your eye on the ball." (Never mind that we're losing market share, if we just keep doing our thing everything will turn out fine.)

- Get rid of your purse. Men manage to get through a day without toting a fourteen pound, leather security blanket. If it is impossible to carry what is needed in jacket pockets then get a briefcase with inside compartments where things can be stowed.

- Don't try to be one of the guys. That ploy cannot be used successfully. Conversely, don't be sexy or cutesy. Men have enough trouble without those complications. Be as attractive as you can in a style of subdued elegance.

- Don't hide your brains.

- Avoid emotionalism at all costs. Do not get furious; a quiet anger is acceptable if directed toward a common enemy: the unscrupulous competition, the incompetent warehouse staff, the bungling computer specialists, etc. A restrained but genuine enthusiasm for the boss's latest idea is the only proper emotion to show. Never, never show tears in public.

- Strive for an air of unruffled determination.
- Use meetings effectively. When in charge:
  1. Have an agenda and stick to it.
  2. Keep attendance as small as possible.
  3. Keep the discussion focused on main issues, not peripheral matters.
  4. Urge everyone to participate.
  5. Reserve your opinions until the end.
  6. Summarize and make a clear decision as to what is the next step.
- When attending a meeting:
  1. Arrive on time but not so early as to be first.
  2. Never offer to get coffee.
  3. Do not offer to take notes or type up the minutes.
  4. Ask clarification questions, "Is it your position that . . .?"
  5. If you don't understand something, say so.
  6. Do not offer the first solution to a problem. First solutions are never adopted unless made by the boss.
  7. Be a synthesizer. Draw together opposing views in a way that is acceptable to all.
  8. Focus on the main issue. Do not be distracted by side issues. Identify the critical elements in a problem and concentrate on them alone.
- Stop smoking. Business people are becoming increasingly suspicious of individuals who cannot shake harmful habits.
- Do not allow your weight to increase significantly. With few exceptions, fat people do not succeed in business.
- Get regular exercise. A business career is mentally fatiguing. In order to function effectively, the mental fatigue must be replaced by physical fatigue.
- Do not drink more than one glass of wine at lunch. There is a double standard in business about drinking. A man may be forgiven for getting high, a woman will not.
- Stay calm and analytical regardless of surrounding turmoil.
- Learn to work quickly but without the appearance of frantic haste.
- Drive a car with skill and a sure sense of direction. Out-of-town trips with rented cars are part of every manager's experience.

- Express decisions in a calm, confident manner, giving the impression that questions will be tolerated but not opposition.

- Be as technically competent as any man in the unit. Do not be bullied into yielding to the supposed superiority of men in technical areas.

- Don't try to be "tough." A firm resolve is just as effective and much more impressive.

- Avoid self-effacement. Good little girls who always do their work and never cause trouble do not get rewarded, they get taken for granted.

- Develop a competitive spirit. Good losers will frequently need to update their resumes.

- Demand everything that your position entitles you to. Do not make the mistake in assuming that the superficial aspects of a position are unimportant. If your position ordinarily carries with it an outside office with a window and a carpet make sure that you get them. The appearance of status is sometimes as important as the reality.

- Do not personalize slights or discriminatory actions. You must view such treatment as aimed at women in general and not you in particular.

- Do not make a scene when faced with discrimination because of your sex. Stay calm and rational but absolutely firm in your resolve not to accept discriminatory treatment.

- Ignore humorous remarks by men that arise from a traditional view of women. The women's struggle will not be won by calling down every man who makes a mother-in-law joke or who tells a story that illustrates the supposed inherent silliness of women.

An ambitious woman in business faces a rough road. You are part of a fierce struggle against a stubborn and resourceful foe. As with any new movement, those who go ahead cutting the trail for others to follow work the hardest, suffer the most, and enjoy fewer of the rewards. You must not only face the foe every day but do so with humor and a sense of proportion intact. Success will only come to those who clearly outdo their competition. You must be smarter, better organized, more dedicated, and with greater perseverance. The rewards are there and I hope they are commensurate with the sacrifices that are required.

3 FIRST TASK

T he first question a new manager asks is, "What do I do now?"
If you are an outsider, new to the department, the wisest course
is to allow the unit to continue to function as before while you
watch, listen, question, and learn. Your first task is to learn the
business of your department. Simultaneously you must learn about
the people who are now reporting to you.

- About the department you will want to know:
    1. What work is being done?
    2. How is the work being done?
    3. Why is it being done in that way?

- About your people you will want to know:
    1. Who are they?
    2. What are their strengths/weaknesses?
    3. What are their motivations?
    4. How do they view themselves?
    5. What are their skill levels?

While you are learning about your new department and its
people you must still handle departmental problems as they occur.
Some of these problems will require action on your part, which

should be taken only when necessary and only after you have considered several courses of action and decided on the most feasible. On matters of any consequence you should consult your boss before announcing any decisions.

You are also likely to find many problems are being brought to you that should be handled directly by the subordinate involved. This "delegation upward" is a result of uncertainty by your subordinates as to what you expect of them. It is also a testing to see how you handle various situations and to give the subordinates an idea of how much they can get away with. On matters that should be handled by subordinates, force them to provide their own solutions to the problems. One of your primary tasks is to develop competency and independence in your subordinates. This effort should begin immediately after you assume the manager's role. Let your people know that you expect them to function without minute by minute guidance from you and that they must accept responsibility for their work.

As a new manager you will be expected to make changes. Do not be rushed into hasty action. Changes should only be implemented after you have developed a thorough understanding of your department and its people. Depending upon the complexity of the business, your learning period can take anywhere from one to six months. Somewhere in that time period you should develop a reasonable grasp on the business of your unit and the capability of your people. Whatever changes you want to make should then be implemented. During the first six months a new manager is in a "honeymoon" period, when changes are accepted with a minimum of resistance from superiors and subordinates. Take advantage of this period to make those difficult decisions that probably should have been made by the previous manager. This is the time to change outmoded procedures and to correct people problems. Unproductive employees should be transferred, put on probation, or terminated. Changes should be made decisively and authoritatively after thorough planning. You will never again have this opportunity to put your stamp on this unit. A manager gets only one "honeymoon" per promotion; don't let it slip away without taking the needed action that everyone expects.

Once your changes have been announced they must be carried out without exception. This is one of the few times that a manager must be inflexible. The only discussion allowed concerns how your changes are to be implemented. There should be no discussion about what is to be done. If you show weakness at this point and allow needed changes to be stalled or side-tracked because of anticipated resistance by the workers you will sacrifice much of the authority you will need to manage your unit properly. Once your decisions are announced firmness is essential. Do not waver and you will save yourself much unnecessary discussion at this time and in the future.

If you have been promoted within your own unit you should already know the business and the people. Presumably you already have some ideas on changes that need to be made. If this is so then strike quickly before any resistance can form. Within the first month you should put together an operating plan that describes the changes you want to make, what you hope to accomplish, and how the plan is to be implemented. As soon as the plan is approved by your boss, it should be announced and implemented as quickly as possible. Again, a firm insistence on the implementation of the plan will save much time and energy in the future.

If you are not certain what changes need to be made, the following chapter on job analysis should be helpful.

EXERCISES

Format For Change

List below, or on a separate sheet of paper, the people in your unit who should be transferred, put on probation, or terminated.

Name	Action to Be Taken	Reason
1.		
2.		
3.		
4.		

List below the activities of your unit that need to be changed or eliminated.

	Activity	Change or Elimination	New or Revised Activity
1.			
2.			
3.			
4.			
5.			

4 JOB ANALYSIS

You've just gotten your first promotion. Where once you were a simple laborer in the vineyards you are now a manager. Instead of being responsible for just your own work you are now responsible for the work of others. Rather than motivate and direct yourself you must now provide that for other people. You will no longer be evaluated on your own productivity but instead on the productivity of the people who report to you. What is now expected of you and your people?

When you were promoted, you were probably given a job description for your new position. The job description was intended to help you understand what was expected of you. Do not be misled by your job description. It describes what you are to do, not what you are to accomplish. It is a listing of activities, not objectives.

"Supervise the operation of the accounts payable department." "Manage and direct the activities of the purchasing department." "Coordinate all activities of the shipping and receiving department." "Direct the activities of all sales reps assigned to your division." "Control all warehouse operations."

What the job description does not tell you is what you are

expected to accomplish. Words such as supervise, manage, and direct are activity words. They describe only general responsibilities. The assumption is that if activities are done, results will be achieved. Not so! Tasks can be merely performed without achieving results. I can start my car and drive until the tank is empty but if the wheels are turned to the left I will continue to drive in a circle. The engine will have been running with all pistons firing up and down, the car will have been in constant motion, and enormous amounts of energy will have been expended, but at the end of it all I will not have gone anywhere. Nothing will have been accomplished in spite of all the activity.

In order for my car to do productive work, I have to decide where I want to go with it (objective), decide how to get there (action plan), and then follow through with my plan (implementation). To succeed in your new job you must set objectives, develop action plans, and then follow through with implementation.

One of your first tasks as a manager is to determine what is expected of you and your unit in terms of results, not activities. If you are part of a large corporation this may not be as easy as it appears. Large organizations tend to lose sight of their goals and focus on activities. Your boss may be of little help as you seek to determine the results that are expected; he/she may have been in one place for so many years that the comfort of repetitive activity has replaced a pursuit of constantly changing goals. Regardless of the orientation of your boss, for your own career growth you must determine the results that either are, or should be, expected of your unit.

With proper direction the identification of goals is not overly difficult. The starting point is the raison d'etre for every business—maximization of profits! The overriding goal is the same for every employee—how to help the company maximize profits. This simple question has two simple answers: increase revenue and reduce costs. Everything you do as a manager should be aimed at one or both of these objectives. Even if you are not in the sales department, you can help increase revenue by striving to improve the quality of your products or your company's service to its customers. You can help cut costs by spending less or by being more productive. Operating your department more efficiently will increase productivity and reduce costs. No matter what type of unit you are responsible for you really have only these two objectives. If you focus on them and not the activities of your unit you will contribute to your company's profitability and therefore your own career growth.

Sometimes it is difficult to determine productivity of staff units. What is the output expected of a personnel department, a finance department, or an operations department? Each of these staff departments provides a service to the sales and manufacturing departments. Measuring the productivity of a staff department is not an easy task. However, with proper job analysis it is possible to develop measures of efficiency even for staff units.

For example, a personnel department can measure output in terms of the average number of days it takes to fill a position. Quality of work can be partially measured by the average number of applicants interviewed per job. (The presumption is that more applicants produce better hires.) The number of internal promotions can be an indicator of the effectiveness of a personnel operation. Costs can be measured by the amounts spent on employment agency fees. Efficiency can be measured by the ratio between the personnel department's headcount and the number of job placements accomplished.

- Operations can measure its performance in many ways:
    1. The ratio between sales and inventory levels.
    2. Average time between receipt of an order and its shipment to the customer.
    3. Percentage of shipments or invoices that contain errors.
    4. Average number of orders processed per clerk each day.
    5. Average shipping costs per order.

- Finance can measure its performance in a number of ways:
    1. The accuracy of cash needs projections.
    2. The timeliness of regular reports.
    3. The number of Days of Sales outstanding in Accounts Receivable.
    4. Measurable cost savings made possible by computerizing routine work.
    5. Improving the return on the short-term investment of company funds.

In every unit of every company there are specific, measurable objectives that, if accomplished, contribute to profitability. These should be the goals of each unit.

The activities of the unit are the means by which goals are accomplished. An effective manager constantly remembers that the activities are a means to an end, not an end in themselves. A competent manager focuses on the goals of the unit and constantly examines activities to ensure that they are contributing to the achievement of those goals.

As a manager one of your first tasks is to identify the goals for your unit. These goals should be specific and measurable. If you have already been provided with such goals by your manager, you are fortunate. More than likely you have been told about general problems revolving around activities and left to discover goals for yourself.

Now stop and develop your unit's goals. In the space provided list the four most important goals of your unit.

1.

2.

3.

4.

Read your listings carefully. Are the goals stated in specific and measurable terms? *Specific* means exact, precise, not vague or amorphous. *Measurable* means having a number attached to it or requiring a physical result that can be seen and touched. If your goals read like this then they need to be reworked: "Efficiently manage the operation of the order entry department." This goal is vague because the operative phrases are not specific. What exactly is meant by "Efficiently ..." or "... manage the operation ..."? The statement is really a job description term and is not suitable as a goal.

More specifically one might say: "Maintain or improve the performance of the order entry department." This objective is specific in the sense that a maintenance or improvement of performance is expected. However, it is not totally specific because it does not identify the performance that is to improve.

Specifically one could say: "Reduce interval between receipt of orders and entry into computer." This is specific in that the manager would know the task ahead. Unfortunately it is not measurable. What is an acceptable reduction, 5 percent, 10 percent, 20 percent? There is no number attached to this goal and it is, therefore, not measurable.

Rewritten it might read: "By April 30th have all orders entered into computer no later than the next day after receipt of each order." Now we have a goal that is specific, measurable, and has a date attached to it. This last point is important because the date forces one to take action and lessens the chance of procrastination.

If your goals were not specific and measurable and did not include a deadline, rework them in the space below.

1.

2.

3.

4.

With your goals firmly established an action plan must be developed to accomplish them. If you are wise you will allow your subordinates to participate in developing the action plans. Although it is a manager's responsibility to set goals, the subordinates must do the work that accomplishes the goals. If they work in a half-hearted way or if they are resentful, the chances of accomplishing the goals are small because goals are more likely to be achieved by willing workers.

One way of securing a willing spirit is to allow subordinates to involve themselves in planning how the work is to be done. Let them help you plan how to accomplish your goals. This will require that you clearly transmit your goals to your subordinates and then ask for their suggestions on how best to accomplish the goals. The solicitation of suggestions can be done either individually or in a group. The method that is most effective will be determined by the personalities and past experiences of your subordinates.

A group meeting works well to build team spirit, and ideas that are presented will often spark others. However, there are factors that may make a group meeting nonproductive:

—A strong minded, talkative subordinate who would dominate the meeting and inhibit the others.

—Personality conflicts that would be disruptive.

—A general timidity or defensiveness that would severely restrict open discussion.

These or other factors may make a group discussion impractical. If so, individual sessions may accomplish most of what is needed. Regardless of the procedure used the manager must be a good listener. Here are some guidelines for eliciting a full range of ideas and winning support.

- State the objective clearly. Outline the problem.

- Do not offer your own ideas to start the ball rolling. Ask for suggestions and wait for responses.

- Listen carefully; take notes if necessary.

- Use follow-up questions to elicit full understanding of each suggestion.

- Encourage full participation.

- Be sensitive to the mood that prevails.

- Do not categorize suggestions as good or bad.

- Summarize to keep the discussion in focus.

- Try to develop a working consensus.

If you are forced into individual meetings with your subordinates it may be necessary at the end to have a group meeting to sum up and develop a consensus.

Once an action plan is agreed upon the manager should see to its implementation. The plan should be broken down into workable parts and one person assigned to each part. Responsibility must be clearly distributed among the subordinates so that each one knows exactly what is expected. The manager then monitors progress to ensure that the plan is on schedule.

An effective manager sets clear goals, develops agreed upon action plans, delegates responsibility for implementation, and regularly monitors progress.

Once you have established objectives and action plans and have assigned responsibility for implementation it is time to step back and look at what it takes to function effectively as a manager. Effectiveness as a manager is a skill that can be acquired; it is not an inherited trait. In almost all cases the effective manager has either learned or developed a personal system for efficient work. Regardless of the job or the industry the systems of effective managers show consistent similarities. Most effective managers concentrate on a few essentials:

- They focus on what is important.

- They continually question what is being done.

- They use time effectively.

- They speculate and experiment.

CONCENTRATE ON WHAT IS IMPORTANT

All managers and their units have responsibilities in a number of areas. If you are a field sales manager, you are responsible for a portion of the company sales. You are also responsible for operating within an assigned budget, penetrating new markets, field testing new products, handling customer complaints, recruiting, hiring and training new personnel, providing customer feedback to the home office, and a host of other responsibilities. If you are an editor, your responsibilities could include identifying possible authors, working with present or future authors, ensuring that manuscripts are received on time, preparing budgets and forecasts for manuscripts, preparing completed manuscripts according to a time schedule, distributing work in an efficient manner within your department, assisting in the training of sales persons, providing input to the marketing and promotion departments, and various other tasks. Aside from this list of responsibilities there are many lesser tasks that require the time and attention of each of the managers involved. A similar listing of responsibilities for managers in other parts of a company would be as long or longer. In fact, if each manager were to list all the tasks that involve his/her time and attention the list would probably run for a number of pages.

Each manager, therefore, is faced with the initial task of determining what is important and what is unimportant. The wise manager knows that it is impossible to give full attention to all possible responsibilities. The effective manager concentrates on those few aspects of the job that are most important, and gives them the most attention. The first and most important question that a manager can ask is, "What needs to be done?"

The effective manager, then, must determine the priority tasks of the unit. It is only then that the manager can begin to consider how to accomplish these tasks. In other words, the first question that a manager asks is, "Where do we want to go?"; this is then followed by, "How do we get there?" In most instances there are probably only four or five separate tasks that, if accomplished, will ensure the success of the manager and the unit.

Take your list of four objectives to your boss and determine through discussion that these indeed should be primary goals of your unit. If changes are necessary make sure that you both agree to them. The end result should be goals that you are both committed to.

QUESTION EVERYTHING

Once the work has been assigned on priority tasks the manager should examine what is being done. He/she should look critically at the way the unit is working and the procedures used in accomplishing the work. One should always be asking, "Why are we doing this?"

The story is told that shortly after Winston Churchill was appointed Prime Minister, he was reviewing the work of an artillery battery. He watched with interest as the vehicles pulled the cannons into position. The artillerymen leaped from their trucks and began the process of loading, aiming, and firing the cannons. Churchill noted that at each cannon there was a man standing at attention just to the right rear who had no apparent responsibility. Churchill asked who the man was and was told that he was the picket. Upon further investigation by the War Office, Churchill learned that the picket was responsible for holding the horses while the cannons were being fired.

As with Churchill, the questioning manager will probably find that some of the tasks and procedures of the unit are done more out of habit than real need. Some things are done in a certain way because they have always been done that way. Other tasks are done that probably shouldn't be done at all merely because nobody has the time or courage to stop them. The laws of inertia apply to the activities of people as well as to the movement of bodies in space. Once an activity begins, it acquires a life and momentum of its own and a strong effort is required to change its course or halt its motion. The effective manager will examine the activities and procedures of the unit in a critical way to determine if it is time for a change.

The principle of zero-based budgeting can be applied in areas other than finance. A revealing question that a manager should ask on a regular basis is, "If we were not doing this today, would we begin it?" If the answer is no, then the manager ought to seriously consider abandoning that particular task or procedure, or perhaps, substituting a more effective means of accomplishing the same objective. Such a task is like the human appendix; it may have had a use at one time but is now merely a source of concern. An effective manager who finds an "appendix" will remove it before it becomes a serious problem.

USE TIME EFFECTIVELY

If as a manager you would like to try a disheartening experience, for one week keep track of exactly how you spend your working time. At the end of the week calculate the total time spent on each task and then match the time spent against the importance of each task. In other words, see if there is a correlation between the importance of a task and the amount of time spent on it. Do not be discouraged by the results. Even the most effective managers find that they spend a disproportionate amount of time on tasks of minor importance. However, the effective manager is aware of this tendency and fights to correct it. It should be obvious that a manager must apportion time where it can do the most good. With few exceptions this means that concentration should be on those tasks that are most critical to the success of the unit. The effective manager knows that there are other pressing calls upon his/her time but yields to those demands as little as possible.

The wise manager makes sure that before turning his/her attention to lower priority responsibilities, the major priorities are well in hand. There are some tasks of a lesser nature that can be ignored completely. There are others that can be cleared up with a few minutes' attention. There are, however, a great many lesser tasks that require attention far in excess of their importance. It is in this area that the greatest danger lies for the manager. The seductiveness of these problems is very strong and the manager who does not resist their pull will spend too much time on minor procedural, administrative, or personnel matters. If these are such that they cannot be ignored, the manager should delegate the resolution of such problems to one or more subordinates. This delegation will accomplish two things. First, it frees the manager to focus on those tasks that are most important, and second, it allows a subordinate to exercise a certain amount of judgment, initiative, and leadership. Both outcomes are highly desirable. A manager's time is a resource along with the other business resources of money, people, and physical equipment. It should be used with as much prudence as any other resource. How a manager uses the resource of time will have a significant impact upon his/her effectiveness.

You should invest your time as wisely and carefully as you would invest your financial or human resources. Just as you would not waste money or the physical equipment of your unit so you should not waste your time or the time of your subordinates. Each day you should be conscious of the limited time available to you and resolve that you and your people will make maximum use of this precious resource.

SPECULATE AND EXPERIMENT

"I'm so busy I don't have time to think." Whether spoken or not this is a feeling that many managers have. These are people who furiously rush from one task to another like hamsters on a treadmill. There is no doubt that energy is being expended and there is considerable activity, but the output of that work is not evident. If the hamster ever thought about it, he might decide to get off the treadmill and take a walk around the cage to see what might be discovered.

A manager is not paid just for *doing*, but also for *thinking*— thinking about what is being done, why it is being done, and how it is being done. You should be thinking about how the work of your unit can be done better, faster, or cheaper. You should be thinking about the goals of the company and your unit's contribution to achieving those goals.

The effective manager should be a speculator. Not a speculator in the commodities market or on Wall Street but a speculator about work and responsibilities. You should be the kind of person who asks, "What if . . .?" You should be constructing hypotheses about activities, unit objectives, subordinates, and assignments. You should be turning over various alternatives to whatever is presently being done and looking at things in a different way. Try to break free of the constraints of the "tunnel vision" that we all develop after we have been in a job for a while. The effective manager is willing to experiment and to take the hypotheses that seem to have merit and to try them out. He/she calculates the effects, both positive and negative and determines when an experiment is justified. The effective manager is aware that the world never stands still. A business never stands still. It is either moving forward, growing, expanding, and becoming more profitable or it is falling, shrinking, and becoming less profitable. Change is the only constant in business as it is in life. The effective manager must be working to accomplish productive change. Neither the unit nor the company can stand still; whatever was done yesterday may not be sufficient reason for doing it today. The markets that the company is focusing on today may no longer exist five or six years from now. Customers are changing and the products of the company must also change.

When I was in college all engineering students were identified immediately by the slide rules that never left their sides. A famous old German company named Keuffel and Esser supplied slide rules to the world. They probably owned as much of the slide rule market as Polaroid owns of the instant camera market. About four years ago Keuffel and Esser stopped making slide rules—the market for them no longer existed. Pocket calculators have completely replaced slide rules in engineering offices and classrooms. I don't know how K & E adapted to the disappearance of their market. I hope they saw it coming and were prepared to enter into, or develop, a new market. If they failed to foresee change coming then they must have suffered some grievous wounds. Business history is full of stories of products that became outdated, manufacturing processes that became obsolete, and markets that changed or disappeared. Change is inevitable. The only question is whether your company will be a victim of change or profit from it.

The effective manager understands that progress requires change, but not all change is progress. Change must be managed without destroying the foundation upon which it is constructed. It is not an easy task to manage a business so that the stability of the old is retained while the promise of the new is being developed. Effective managers are speculators and experimenters but they act so the change that actually occurs is gradual and continual rather than abrupt and traumatic.

He that will not apply new remedies must expect new evils: for time is the greatest innovator.—Francis Bacon

There is nothing permanent, except change.—Heraclitus

EXERCISES

1. List the five most important responsibilities you have as a manager.

1.

2.

3.

4.

5.

2. List five lesser responsibilities that can be delegated to a subordinate.

1.

2.

3.

4.

5.

3. List three procedures or tasks you should investigate to determine whether or not they are obsolete.

1.

2.

3.

4. List three possible hypotheses you have about making your unit more productive. After each hypothesis list the means by which you would test it.

Hypothesis	Means Of Testing
1.	1.
2.	2.
3.	3.

5 CREATIVE THINKING

People in and out of business suffer from a number of misconceptions about creative thinking. The impression exists that creative thinking is done solely by long-haired, eccentric geniuses, who think in mysterious ways and speak in obscure phrases. Many companies foster this misconception by isolating their research and development people in laboratories far removed from the everyday business affairs of the company. IBM has its principal research center set on a hilltop about forty miles north of New York City. Each researcher has a small cubicle with a blackboard but no windows. The corridors are on the outside of the building and claim the outside windows. This arrangement is apparently designed to forestall disputes over who gets an office with a window. It may also have been felt that the sylvan view of woods and meadow would prove distracting. The effect is not only to isolate the research staff from the rest of the company, but also from one another.

On Madison Avenue there is a commonly used phrase in which the account executive says to the client, "I'll turn this over to the creative guys and see what they come up with." In other words, "We business people have nothing to do with creativity." Outside the world of business many of us think of creative people as unstable authors living lives of alcoholism and infidelity, or of artists so obsessed by their work and so driven by their monumental egos that they are unable to establish normal relationships with other people, or of effeminate designers and choreographers who live in a bizarre world of flaming temperament and hourly emotional crises.

The belief that creative people are a special breed, distinct from the rest of us, does a disservice to every intelligent person. Creativity is just as essential to the success of a lawyer, an accountant, a doctor, or a business person as it is to any of the practitioners of the fine arts. In any field what usually distinguishes the person of accomplishment from one who never rises above mediocrity is the ability to employ creative thinking in a useful and constructive way. In a successful, well-run business there is as much creative thinking as in the production of a Broadway musical, the development of a new invention, or the writing of a book. Creative thinking, in reality, is problem solving in innovative, unorthodox, and inventive ways. No business can succeed without creative problem solvers applying their talents to the problems of that business.

Every day in the business world creative people are devising unusual answers to problems facing their companies. Most of these innovative solutions go unnoticed by the world in general and frequently by people within the same company. The creative thinker in business is too busy solving the problems of the job and getting things done to look to the world for applause and fame. All of us enjoy the benefits of creative thinking as applied in the business world, yet few of us know to whom we are indebted for those benefits.

Sometime before World War II, Alfred Krupp, the head of the giant German steel company, was advised by one of his production supervisors about a recurring problem in one of the steel mills. Krupp went to investigate and upon arriving at the mill discovered that many of the sheets of steel were coming off the production line with ripples running the full width of the sheet. Krupp and the various people involved spent some time discussing what was causing this rippling effect and ways in which it might be corrected. While examining the defective steel, Krupp suddenly realized that the ripples corresponded to the curvature that is ordinarily given to spoons and forks. Krupp pointed this out to one of the production people and suggested that rather than trying to correct the ripples they use the defective steel to shape tableware. The results were a success and the stainless steel flatware industry was born.

About 1940, a young patent lawyer, Chester Carlson, became

interested in the problem of producing plain paper copies of the many patent applications and legal papers that he had to use in his work. Fortunately he had training in physics and was able to apply his science background to this problem, eventually developing a cumbersome machine that, nevertheless, produced acceptable copies from original documents. It was obvious that in order to make this process marketable, extensive development work would have to be done to reduce the size of the machine, increase the speed of reproduction, and improve the quality of the copies. Carlson took his invention to every major office equipment manufacturer in the United States, including IBM, Smith-Corona, and Remington Rand, and was turned down by all of them. The stated reason was that there was no way of knowing if the machine could ever be perfected, and if it were, how large a market, if any, existed for such a product.

Fortunately for Carlson and for the business world he persisted in his efforts, eventually interesting Joseph Wilson, the president of Haloid Corporation, in his process. With the assistance of the Batelle Institute, Joe Wilson and Haloid eventually produced the first dry-copying machine that could use ordinary paper. Haloid Corporation became Xerox Corporation and Chester Carlson's original copier became the single most profitable product ever manufactured in the United States.

The significance of both of these accomplishments is that they solved a specific problem. Creative thinking does not exist in isolation. It is almost always in response to a particular problem. No one with any sense would sit down and say, "I'm going to begin thinking creatively." That sort of activity would lead nowhere. Until the problem is brought into focus, creative thinking is only speculation. The problem provides the starting point for the creative process. It is not an abstract exercise, it is an attempt to find an answer to a specific problem.

The first step then, in creative thinking, is to identify the problem. The problem provides the outlet and the focus for whatever creative thinking is required to solve it. An interesting business problem was faced a few years ago by the person responsible for marketing a new line of kitchen containers that were designed to be used to store leftover food and other items. The problem in this instance was not the development or the production of the kitchen containers because that had been already accomplished, but rather, how to market and distribute them. For many companies, marketing and distribution are the critical elements in the success or failure of a new product.

The marketing manager considered a number of alternatives,

among them distributing the containers through a network of brokers or distributors who would place them in dime stores, variety stores, and supermarkets. The marketing manager was not satisfied with this solution because this product would be competing directly with many other better known and better established products. His product had a higher price tag and he was not confident of his ability to compete at the store level. While considering this problem, the marketing manager decided to stop thinking about the product and to begin thinking about his customer, the homemaker. He began to consider how to reach that person in ways other than through displays in stores. He thought of the experience of the Fuller Brush Company, which had sales people calling directly upon homemakers, offering them a range of household items and enjoying considerable sales success. He rejected this solution because his product line was not broad enough to support full-time salespersons. The marketing manager then asked himself, if selling to one person at a time was not cost effective, might it be better to sell to a group of people all at one time? The answer to that question was yes. But now the marketing manager was faced with the problem of gathering together groups of people to listen to sales presentations for kitchen containers.

The manager's knowledge of human behavior provided the answer. He knew people enjoyed getting together for social reasons and that virtually any excuse was sufficient under some circumstances to bring people together. He, therefore, devised the idea of a "party," where homemakers would meet together in the residence of one of their neighbors, enjoy some coffee and cake, and as a by-product hear a sales presentation about new kitchen items that might prove of interest to them. The outcome of that idea has made Tupperware one of the most successful and profitable companies in its field.

Another person faced a marketing problem and solved it in a different way. The book business has suffered, and still suffers, from distribution problems. Publishers of hardbound books spend considerable time trying to devise ways to get their products in front of more people. The number of bookstores in this country is extremely limited and the number of people who go into those bookstores is even more limited.

Some years ago a man decided that there was a market for low-cost paperback editions of recent books. This man felt that inexpensive paper-covered editions of such books, while they were still current, could sell in substantial numbers. He was faced with an essential problem: How to generate enough volume so that the price per book could be kept low. The idea of inexpensive paperback books was not new, but had been around for many years in the publishing industry. Other lines of low-cost softbound books were already being published. The difficulty with these editions was that since their only exposure was in bookstores, the volume of sales was low and the profit margins were correspondingly low. It was not a particularly profitable business.

The man with the idea in this case decided that the only way to generate significant business for his new paperback line was to stop thinking of them as books to be distributed in the traditional manner and to begin thinking of them in other ways. He finally decided that the only sensible way to think of these paperback books was to consider them magazines and to distribute them accordingly. Now his potential market was not limited to those people who entered a bookstore but included everybody who entered a variety store, a dime store, a drug store, a supermarket, an airline, bus, or train terminal, or anywhere else that magazines were sold. The ease of access to the paperbound books and their low cost made them an immediate success and gave birth to an industry that today generates far more revenue than the sales of hardcover books.

There is a significant similarity between the story of Tupperware and the story of Pocket Books Inc. It is a similarity shared by almost every creative idea—the solution of a problem often turns out to be a new combination of two older ideas.

Most creative thinking is not creative in the sense that it discovers something that no one has ever thought of, or anticipated, and that is completely divorced from all prior concepts. The chance to invent the wheel or anything comparable is pretty much a thing of the past. Almost all creative thinking involves taking two heretofore unrelated ideas and combining them to form a new idea. This is the process Arthur Koestler calls "bisociation." Bisociation is the essence of creative thinking. It is a synthesis of two or more disparate ideas that forms one new idea. Tupperware took the concept of socialization and the idea of selling directly into the home to make a new idea, the Tupperware "party." The people at Pocket Books Inc. took the two ideas of inexpensive paperback reprints and magazine distribution, and put them together to create a new industry.

Bisociation has an ancient and honorable history. The story is told that Gutenberg had been puzzling over the problem of mechanical printing for a considerable period of time. One day he happened to see a wine press in operation and suddenly saw how that principle could be applied to automatic printing. He had already been toying with the idea of typesetting in a primitive form. He combined that idea with the wine press, and invented the first practical printing press.

Let us accept that creativity is possessed by everyone of intelligence. The question then becomes, "How can this creativity be released and brought to bear upon the problems that each manager faces?" In order to apply creative thought, one must be conscious of its existence and purposefully seek to utilize it. This is one of the essential characteristics of a good manager, a constant questioning attitude about everything he/she is involved with, especially those things that are most taken for granted.

In order to think creatively certain elements are essential. First, the problem must be clearly defined. Be sure that the problem you are focusing on is the real problem and not simply a symptom of a deeper ailment. For example, a headache may be due to tension, to a brain tumor, or to any number of other causes. Treating the headache with aspirin, tranquilizers, or narcotics may relieve the symptoms but will do nothing to correct the underlying cause. So a manager who assumes that a production falloff means that the assembly line workers are simply not working hard enough, and seeks to correct that problem by driving them harder, may be treating the symptoms rather than the problem. The problem may very well be antiquated equipment, or inefficient flow, or improper supervision, or any of a host of other reasons. The perceptive manager will ascertain the true problem and not be misled by symptoms posing as a problem.

The second step in thinking creatively is to begin thinking and using words that are as specific as possible. The more specific one can be in the description and analysis of the problem, and in the construction of possible alternatives, the more likely it is that a practical solution will emerge. Avoid generalities as much as possible and continually attempt to refine your thinking in as specific and detailed a manner as possible. Remember that we can only think using the words that are available to us. The words we select should be direct rather than vague. A creative problem solver may begin by using general terms, but quickly narrows the focus. For example, a sales manager may say, "We have to increase sales this year by ten percent." The wise sales manager does not begin an analysis or discussion of this problem by considering how total company sales might be increased by ten percent, but is much more likely to arrive at a practical answer, or answers, by considering what can be done at the regional level, the district level, and the level of the individual salesperson. At each one of those levels specific ideas can be generated that can result in increased sales, the cumulative effect of which will be to achieve the company goal.

In late 1976, it became known that Ohio parochial schools would receive somewhere between 18 and 20 million dollars in state aid that had previously not been available. The sales manager for a small publishing subsidiary of a communications company set a sales goal of $500,000 for 1977, the first year in which the money would be available. In analyzing the problem, the manager quickly realized that given the number of parochial schools in the state of Ohio, and the area to be covered, there was no way that his one sales representative could call upon each of these potential customers. His solution was similar to that of the Tupperware company. He decided that rather than try to sell the schools individually he would sell them in groups. The problem then became, "How does one gather together parochial school educators from a large area in one central place, and have them listen to sales presentations?" Obviously, few people will go out of their way solely for the purpose of hearing a sales presentation. The manager decided that if he could bring together the people with the power to make buying decisions he could justify providing them with a free dinner. He knew this offer would bring him a number of people. He also decided that a cocktail hour before dinner would draw additional people. If he had stopped there, the campaign probably would have met with a reasonable amount of success. The manager wanted, however, to come up with something extra that would ensure the success of his meeting. He expanded the horizon of his thinking and produced a creative answer. It seemed to the manager that there were resources within the parent corporation, CBS, Inc., that could be of assistance to him. As a communications company with television and record divisions, he knew that there were many CBS employees who were nationally known, in whom people had an interest, and who could provide the extra inducement to make his meetings a success. The result was four meetings across Ohio; in Toledo, Cleveland, Columbus, and Cincinnati, where selected parochial school administrators and teachers were invited to a dinner, a cocktail hour, and were given an opportunity to hear and talk to either Hughes Rudd or Charles Kuralt. Naturally before the dinner and the main speaker were provided, the educators listened to presentations of the company products. The four meetings were an outstanding success with up to 450 people attending each one of them. The final result was that instead of sales of $500,000, the actual sales for the year amounted to over $1,500,000.

The most interesting aspect of this story is that the problem to be solved was in reality an opportunity that is sometimes easy to see. However, the problem that Alfred Krupp faced was also an opportunity. He was the only one perceptive enough to see the possibilities within the rippled steel; everyone else considered it simply a problem to be eliminated and overcome. There are few problems in business that are not at the same time opportunities. The manager who can see the opportunity inherent in a problem and seize upon and take maximum advantage of it will move rapidly up through the ranks of the company.

To think creatively one must avoid becoming too orderly in one's thought processes. Orderliness is a valuable attribute, but it can lead to rigidity. Occasional sessions of brainstorming, either by oneself or with an associate, can be some of the most productive time that a manager can spend. Don't be afraid to conceive of daring, original, unorthodox ideas. Admittedly, many of those ideas will be too risky to pursue, but every manager should be open to that type of creative thinking, and look for the occasional, startling idea that can make a significant difference.

In most instances, creative thinking is enhanced by having another person with whom you can exchange views. This person need not be someone within your company or familiar with your job. Sometimes that person can serve as an idea stimulator, or may simply serve as a sounding board, giving you an opportunity to hear your thoughts as you express them. As you express your ideas you will find yourself refining them, considering aspects that had not occurred to you before, and many times developing alternative solutions that had not previously appeared.

Brainstorming is a process by which the creative powers in a group of people can be unleashed. When used properly it will provide many possible solutions to a problem, most of which would not have been developed without the brainstorming approach. Alex Osborn coined the term brainstorming and in his book, *Applied Imagination* (Scribner's, 1963), shows how companies can tap the creative imagination of employees to help solve company problems.

Many companies have employee suggestion programs to encourage the generation of useful ideas, but such programs are passive in nature. Brainstorming is an *active* process in which managers bring together groups of employees to focus on particular problems. It is a strategy whereby a problem is attacked by a barrage of ideas. The purpose is to generate as many ideas as possible with no thought given to practicality. The wildest and most outrageous ideas are encouraged because often they will spark an innovative idea that might otherwise not be thought of. In a typical thirty minute session it is not unusual for forty to fifty ideas to be generated, of which four or five will be both practical and innovative.

A brainstorming session should consist of five to seven persons plus a leader; six is usually considered an ideal number. Participants should be invited, not forced to attend. They can be from the same or different departments or job categories. Having at least one person from outside the group will usually produce ideas that are different from the rest. The session should last for no more than thirty to forty minutes, during which the leader should not attempt to control the flow of ideas. The leader's function is to stimulate the production of ideas and many times will have to offer outrageous proposals to get the group thinking in unorthodox ways. The leader is also responsible for writing each idea on a flip chart or blackboard where they are clearly visible. Finally, the leader must prevent the use of inhibiting comments such as "We've tried that." or "It will cost too much." or "We don't work that way." or "The boss will never buy that."

After all ideas are listed they are evaluated and the five or six most promising are submitted for consideration to the person faced with the problem. In the evaluation great care must be taken not to eliminate unusual ideas solely because they are different. Unorthodox ideas should only be eliminated when demonstrably impractical because of cost, time, or other limiting factors.

The rules of brainstorming are:
1. Every idea suggested is listed.
2. No evaluation of ideas is permitted.
3. Let your imagination run free.
4. Use one idea to spark others.
5. Don't worry about the practicality of an idea.
6. The more ideas, the better.

A recent article points out the importance of communication in developing new ideas.

White collar productivity is also crucial at Corning since the corporation depends heavily on bright, innovative scientists and engineers. The company hopes to improve the productivity of the corporate engineering people by bringing them together under one roof in a new building. The coffee lounges will be equipped with blackboards to encourage the engineers to talk out technical problems with each other. Escalators will be installed instead of elevators, to facilitate movement from floor to floor and make face-to-face communication easier.[1]

Finally, do not hurry. Do not try to force solutions when they are not forthcoming naturally. Many of our most creative ideas require a silent period of gestation. We have all experienced those occasions when an answer, a solution, or an insight suddenly pops into our mind. Although it comes forth unbidden from our subconscious it always results from previous consideration or analysis of a particular problem. Often these sudden solutions come to us when we are physically relaxed and our minds have shifted into neutral. For many people that period is just before falling asleep or just after waking up in the morning. But whenever it is, (and each one of us has his/her own time when these insights appear) don't try to hurry the process. Remember, however, that it is not enough to wait for inspiration to strike because it will appear only after thought and analysis have taken place. Before a solution can be found the problem must be clearly defined and its parameters established.

Creative thinking is a talent that each one of us possesses. It is a resource that lies within us waiting to be called forth; a silent servant standing beside us, waiting to come to our aid. Use this resource, understand and develop this talent, and in the process make yourself a better manager and your company a more profitable enterprise.

EXERCISES

List below a problem you face that would be suitable for a brainstorming session. Define the problem as specifically as possible. Be prepared for further refinement of the problem when the group begins to work on it.

Problem

List below six persons you plan to invite to the session:

1.

2.

3.

4.

5.

6.

List the place where you want to hold the session. It must be conducive to a free flow of ideas. (The board room may be too inhibiting.)

Place:

Date:

Time:

Follow up:

Unless something happens as a result of the session it will be a waste of everyone's time. Whatever the outcome, it should be relayed to the participants so they know there was some purpose to their efforts.

NOTE

1. "How Three Companies Increased Their Productivity," *Fortune*, March 10, 1980.

6 PROBLEM ANALYSIS

Problem analysis is one part of the process by which a manager evaluates a situation, determines a course of action, implements a program to accomplish a specific objective, and provides a monitoring system to determine whether or not the objective is being met. The three essential elements of this process are the analysis of the problem, the making of the decision, and the implementation of the action plan to accomplish the objective. Viewed in that context, it is apparent that problem analysis and decision making should not be considered in isolation. Each is essential to the eventual resolution of the problem and accomplishment of the objective. Although a separation is made between problem solving in this chapter and decision making in the next chapter, it should be understood that in real life these two activities do not exist independently, but are integral parts of the same process.

Most managers find that the major portion of their workday is spent solving problems. Whether these are problems involving people, physical resources, productivity, or budgets, a manager is faced with an unending succession of problems that must be met and solved. There are many ways of solving problems. For some managers, the almost irresistible tendency is to apply those solutions that have been used in the past. For some repetitive problems this is a satisfactory procedure. One of the advantages of experience is that it allows one to draw upon the solutions of the past and apply them to present day situations. Assuming that history is repeating itself, the solutions will in many cases result in effective action. Other managers may apply intuition or hunches to solve problems. A manager using this approach successfully will need intuitive powers bordering on the supernatural. Past experience or intuition can occasionally provide satisfactory solutions. However, long term, consistently effective problem solving requires a process that can be relied upon when experience is inadequate and intuition fails.

One of the significant trends in modern business is an attempt to make the process of problem analysis and decision making more rational, more objective, more quantitative, and less intuitive. The effective manager seeks to apply a rational, logical approach to problem analysis. It is apparent that adeptness in problem analysis is not an inborn trait but rather a skill that can be acquired by any intelligent, diligent person. The steps to effective decision making are simple to learn and, when applied effectively, can greatly reduce the risks involved.

DEFINE THE PROBLEM

The first and most important step in the problem solving process is an accurate evaluation of the problem. An effective manager must be like an accomplished physician who is able to observe the symptoms of an ailment, but not mistake those symptoms for the disease itself. The skilled physician will find beneath the symptoms the true cause of the patient's affliction. So an effective manager will be able to look past the immediate, visible evidence of a problem to the actual cause itself. The ability to distinguish the nonessential aspects of a situation and penetrate directly to the crux of the problem is a skill not easily acquired. It is not enough for a manager to be solving problems; the effective manager solves the *right* problems. These are not always the most obvious problems.

Solving the wrong problem not only does not get at the basic problem, but usually compounds the difficulty inherent in the situation. In 1967, textbook publishers found themselves in the enviable position of having customers with more money than they knew what to do with. That year was the first in which federal funds were available to the public schools of this country. In fact, in the late spring and early summer of 1967 the schools actually found themselves with two years of funding, because of delays in the first year's appropriations and the speed with which the second year's appropriations were made. The result was a bonanza for publishers of educational materials. During the summer of 1967, orders began pouring into companies that supplied instructional materials to schools. One of those companies, located in Chicago, had a backlog of unprocessed orders that made it difficult to walk through the order processing department, where aisles were clogged with boxes of open orders. The situation continued until late summer of 1967 with the company unable to make a substantial reduction in the number of unprocessed orders. Since this company was a subsidiary of a large corporation, the corporation decided to send down one of its most efficient order processing specialists, with full authority to correct the problem.

The specialist analyzed the problem and came to an immediate decision: "Process all one line orders first; next process all two line orders; next all three line orders, and so on until all the orders have been cleared." There were some objections made by the managers of the company but they were not in a position to effectively resist the commands of the specialist from corporate headquarters. The specialist's decision did result in a gradual reduction of the number of unprocessed orders. By the time school opened just after Labor Day the number of unprocessed orders had been substantially reduced, all that were left were the large orders with many, many lines on them. The specialist could proudly report that the number of unprocessed orders had been reduced to a manageable size. What the specialist had not considered was the impact of his decision upon the customer. The net result was that any customer who had ordered one copy of one book, or one set of colored pencils, or one teacher's manual, received it well in advance of the opening of school. Those schools that had ordered complete sets of the mathematics program for their students, or who had ordered substantial quantities of other basic instructional materials found that those materials did not arrive until four to six weeks after the opening of school. The fury of the customers can well be imagined.

The difficulty was that the specialist treated the symptom and not the problem. The real problem was not to reduce the number of unprocessed orders but, rather, to provide the schools with the products or materials that were most essential to them. Unfortunately, the specialist's answer to the problem was no answer at all, but merely aggravated the basic problem. A problem must be properly defined before it can be successfully solved.

DEVELOP ALTERNATIVES

Once a problem has been properly defined as the essential problem and not a side issue, the next step is to develop a series of alternative solutions. At this stage, these should be considered only hypothetical possibilities and not the only choices available. The aim is to develop as many alternative solutions as possible. The most common weakness in the problem solving skill of managers is to grab the first alternative that sounds reasonable and run with it. Impatience, time pressure, or a crisis should not prevent one from stopping for a few minutes to develop additional alternatives. After experience in hundreds of problem solving situations, I can almost guarantee that the first alternative offered will not be the best. Take the time to develop alternative solutions! Brainstorming sessions with a small group of associates, no more than seven, can be an effective means of providing a wide range of possible answers to the problem. Those solutions should then be critically analyzed and the ones that are not feasible removed from the list. Those that remain should represent possible working solutions to the problem.

GATHER DATA

The third step is to gather the data essential to a thorough analysis of the problem. As each of the possible alternatives is assessed, the need for pertinent information should become clear and the investigator should list all the essential data that are necessary for an objective appraisal of the problem. Much of the information needed may be readily available, some of it may take digging and research to develop, but the decision should not be made until all the relevant data have been established.

In the collecting of data a manager will be presented with a great deal of information. Much of it will come in the form of oral reports from subordinates and others. The wise manager will be suspicious of reports that are not supported by independent data. The experienced manager knows that people have a tendency to make statements of fact that are really opinions. This is done out of a desire to appear more knowledgeable or it can also be an attempt to conceal error. Regardless of the cause, a prudent manager does not accept statements at face value. One of the most effective managers I know asks, "How do you know that?", when faced with a dubious statement. If the statement cannot be supported by evidence, that will become quickly apparent. A subordinate faced with that embarrassment will not usually repeat the error.

"How do you know that?" is a question every manager should employ to ensure getting valid, reliable data on which to base a decision. Josh Billings once said "It ain't what a man don't know that makes him a fool, but what he does know that ain't so."

It should be noted, however, that with most problems of significance and many of lesser substance, frequently all the facts desired are not available. In fact, in almost any problem solving situation one can list data that would be helpful but are not available. The effective manager realizes that in the final analysis most decisions are made on the basis of a judgmental weighing of the facts that are available, and those facts do not always provide 100 percent of the data that could affect the decision. In the end it is the judgment of the manager that is critical. This does not mean that because all the facts cannot be ascertained it is a waste of time to attempt to gather as much information as possible. Even though the information is less than complete it nevertheless provides the framework on which the decision is based. If nothing else it narrows the field of speculation and uncertainty for the manager.

EVALUATE POSSIBILITIES

The next step is an evaluation of the alternative solutions, based on the accumulation of the necessary data. The data and the solutions should be matched together and those solutions that are inconsistent with the data should be discarded. The solutions remaining should then be evaluated on the basis of the type and degree of risk inherent in each decision. The solution to any problem always involves risk and uncertainty. A manager in seeking a solution to a problem must be reconciled to the fact that the solution eventually decided upon will be based on less than total information. There will be risks inherent in that decision, and there will be uncertainties as to the possible consequences. A good manager will attempt to foresee the possible consequences and to develop contingency plans based upon their actually occurring.

In order to function effectively a manager must be willing to accept risks. A manager who is not a risk taker is simply not a manager but an impediment to the company, a deterrent to the people who report to him/her, and a source of embarrassment to the boss. This does not mean that managers should be reckless or hasty in their decisions, but they must accept the risk-taking nature of their responsibilities.

DECIDE UPON ONE ALTERNATIVE

The final step is the determination of the one most feasible solution to the problem. This solution should accommodate as much as possible the data available, the consequences of that particular course of action, and the acceptance and knowledge of risks involved. The final step in this process is the implementation of the decision and the monitoring of the progress of the action plan decided upon. That part of the process will be considered in the next chapter on decision making.

In approaching any problem the role of the manager should be essentially that of a questioner. It is a truism that if the right questions are asked usually the right answer will evolve. At every stage in the process the manager should be questioning, probing, weighing, and evaluating. Questions should be directed at the alternatives, to the data, to the nature of the problem, to the consequences of proposed alternatives, to the risks involved, and to the methods of implementation.

A recent article in the *Wall Street Journal* (February 21, 1980) describes a Japanese technique to develop practical answers to production problems.

> Deeply troubled by slumping productivity, a growing number of major American companies are copying what many management experts believe is the key to Japan's productivity gains: small groups of employees that meet regularly and are trained to spot and solve production problems in their areas.
>
> The groups, called "quality circles," are meeting regularly at 65 companies, up from only 15 a year ago. Companies using the circles include General Motors, Ford Motor, Northrop, Rockwell International, International Harvester and American Airlines.
>
> Most companies say that involving employees in management decisions results in both increased productivity and cost savings. Northrop, the Los Angeles aircraft maker, says it's getting at least a two-for-one return on the cost of maintaining its circles.
>
> The basic idea of the quality circle is quite simple. A plant steering committee, composed of labor and management, decides which area of a company could benefit from a circle. Eight to ten workers are asked to serve on a circle; they meet once a week on company time with their immediate supervisor and with a person trained in personnel or industrial relations. This specialist trains the workers in elementary data-gathering and in statistics. The circle members learn how to talk the language of management

and to present their ideas to executives using such business-school methods as "histograms" and "scatter diagrams."

When a circle believes it has come up with a solution to a problem, it passes it on to management. There have been few instances where management hasn't accepted a circle's recommendations.

This technique recognizes that wisdom and creativity are not the sole provinces of managers. The quality circle uses the creative and analytical powers of all employees and not just managers. Whether you are analyzing a problem alone or in a group, certain basic questions should always be asked. Among them are:

1. What appears to be the problem?

2. Is it the real problem, or is it merely a symptom of a deeper, more serious problem?

3. What are the factors that affect this problem?

4. What are some of the things that might be done to solve the problem?

5. Which of these possibilities appear to be unworkable?

6. What information is needed before a solution can be decided upon?

7. Now that we have the information that is needed are there other alternatives that appear feasible?

8. Of the alternatives available, which seem to be the most feasible?

9. Of those that seem to be the most feasible, what are the risks in each, and what are the uncertainties in each?

10. Of the possible alternatives remaining what are the requirements for manpower and time?

11. Which one solution appears to be the best among the alternatives?

12. What is the best way to implement this solution?

13. How can the action plan developed to implement the solution be monitored and controlled?

At all stages during analysis of the problem the manager should be questioning the validity of the data submitted and the reliability of the source of data. The process by which the problem was defined and the feasibility of each alternative should be questioned, as should every aspect of each step. The questions should be precise, probing, and specific, not vague, general, or abstract. Clarity of thought will lead to clarity of decision and clarity of implementation. Sloppy thought processes will inevitably lead to a careless, sloppy decision that is inadequately implemented.

EXERCISES

In the spaces below analyze one serious problem that you are now facing.

Problem defined:

Overt manifestations of problem:

Apparent causes of problem:

Possible solutions:

1.

2.

3.

4.

Relevant data:

A.

B.

   C.

   D.

   E.

   F.

   G.

Other possible solutions:

   1.

   2.

Most feasible alternative:

Consequences if alternative is adopted:

Costs of adopting alternative:

   • *Money*

   • *Manpower*

   • *Time*

   • *Physical resources*

7DECISION MAKING

A decision is a choice between two or more alternatives. Sometimes the most important decision is determining whether to do something or nothing. Every manager should understand that doing nothing is also a decision, and is many times the best policy. However, when action is necessary alternatives are essential. Decision making is the process by which the one most feasible alternative is selected. It is not usually a matter of finding the one right answer from among all the other wrong answers. Most often, there is more than one alternative that will provide a satisfactory solution to a problem. An effective decision maker is able to select the most effective alternative from among those available.

For example, an art director is frequently faced with choosing a book jacket from a number of possibilities. The decision will have a significant impact on the sale of the book. However, the final decision will not be based on which one cover will add to the sales of the book, and which ones would detract from sales. Any covers that might adversely affect sales should have been eliminated during a preliminary screening process. The actual requirement is to select from a number of good covers the one that is best. Effective decisions are of this nature—selecting the best alternative from among those that are feasible.

A frequent complaint about an ineffective manager is that "He just doesn't seem to be able to make a decision." Often such a manager is unable to make a decision because of a fear of making the wrong decision. Such paralysis of will can be alleviated if it is understood that proper decision making involves choosing from a number of alternatives, each of which is "right."

If there is a secret to effective decision making, it involves reaching a point where all considered alternatives are "right" and the manager can select the one that appears to be best. Then whichever alternative is selected, a reasonably effective outcome will result. The effective decision maker employs a systematic process to produce workable alternatives and to weigh the consequences of implementing each of them.

A systematic process for decision making will, over the long run, produce better decisions than if they are based on hunches or intuition. This does not mean that decision making can be refined into a mechanical or mathematical process whereby one best answer automatically appears. In choosing one alternative to implement, a manager will have to depend upon personal judgment. Subjectivity is still a part of decision making, but it should be only a part, not the whole. A systematic process of decision making will narrow the areas of uncertainty and screen out inappropriate alternatives.

Decision making is the next to last step in problem solving. The initial steps of defining the problem, developing alternatives, and gathering data were described in Chapter 6, Problem Analysis. However, the importance of developing several alternatives needs to be stressed.

The major weakness in the decision making process of ineffective managers is failure to develop a number of alternatives. Their usual procedure is to examine the first alternative that comes to mind and go with it if no immediate flaws appear. If flaws do appear, another alternative is sought and examined in the same way. The second alternative is implemented if no visible flaws appear. If a second alternative is not feasible a third is sought and so on. While this process may produce consideration of a number of alternatives, the alternatives are not measured against one another. The one that is implemented is the first one that appears feasible, with other possibilities never considered. For decision making to be effective, a number of alternatives must be developed before they are evaluated. The wise manager will focus on the development of a wide variety of alternatives, without judging any, until all have been gathered. A recent article highlights the differences between the decision making process in Japan and the United States.

> Unlike American managers whose decisions typically focus on the merits of a single option and whose concerns are more tactical than strategic, the Japanese take great care first to define the precise nature of the issue at hand. Only then do they methodically review every available course of action. Though this process consumes a great deal of time, it ensures that the decision finally reached has been pre-sold. With such a consensus established, every concerned manager knows what the decision is, what it means, and what is necessary to make it work.
>
> By contrast, American managers do not as a rule discipline themselves to consider all possible alternatives. More important, they do not regularly force themselves to think through the kind of issue it is that confronts them. As a result their decisions often address symptoms and nearly always have to be "sold" after the fact. Though the compromises made are roughly comparable to those implicit in any Japanese consensus, they are structurally deficient in a way the Japanese ones are not. Coming after the fact, American compromises and the inevitable trade-offs they involve can play havoc with the systematic logic of the original decision; coming before the fact, Japanese compromises are by definition included—and accounted for—within the decision itself.[1]

Obviously this lengthy process should not be applied to every decision. But even with minor decisions it is worthwhile to take a few minutes to consider other alternatives before forging ahead. Obviously, the amount of time spent in developing alternatives should have a reasonable relationship to the importance of the decision.

It is at this stage that a manager's creativity is most important. The creative manager will allow imagination to produce alternatives that are not just repetitive or traditional. Innovative alternatives will be sought so that when the process of elimination begins there will be a broad spectrum of choices. Most managers find it helpful to use others in developing a variety of alternatives. Discussing a problem with someone else will usually produce ideas that would not have occurred to one person alone. The other person need not be someone with whom the manager works or who is familiar with the manager's job. Many times someone from another field will produce a train of thought that would not occur to a manager who is beginning to succumb to "tunnel vision." After thorough evaluation, the manager will most likely be faced with three or four alternatives, any one of which is a "right" decision. It is at this point that a manager uses judgment to select the alternative that is most right. Experience and an understanding of business and people will increase a manager's batting average in selecting the best alternative. However, even an inexperienced manager will produce workable solutions if a systematic process is followed.

The critical elements in problem solving and decision making are defining the problem and developing alternatives. However, there are other aspects that should not be neglected, which revolve around clarifying objectives and implementation of the decision.

WHAT IS TO BE ACCOMPLISHED

In weighing alternatives to arrive at a decision, the manager should have a carefully thought out understanding of what is to be accomplished by the decision. The process of defining the original problem does not automatically describe the objective to be attained. The manager should have a clear, specific objective in mind.

WHAT FACTORS ARE TO BE CONSIDERED

In arriving at a decision, certainly one of any consequence, it is almost always helpful to write out the considerations that will affect that decision. Those considerations should then be ranked in order of importance. In considering the alternatives, each alternative should be measured against the considerations affecting the decision with more weight given to those ranked at the top of the list. In certain decisions, one primary consideration will outweigh all others so that other factors should receive little or no attention. For instance a manager may have to make a decision knowing that it cannot involve hiring more people. That one factor may largely determine the decision. Usually, however, many factors will affect a decision and listing them allows them to be ranked in importance.

To summarize the process, the manager clearly defines the objective, lists the factors or considerations that have a bearing upon the decision, considers the consequences of each alternative, matches the alternatives to the factors, and then decides upon the most feasible alternative. As written, this appears to be a very sequential, orderly, almost inevitable process. In reality the manager is almost always faced with certain unknowns. There are unknowns among the data that have been assembled; there is almost never total information available about any particular problem. One must live with the knowledge that there may be other aspects of the situation that are either unknown or for which the assessment of their importance is not accurate. The biggest unknown, of course, is the effect of the decision upon the people who will be affected by it.

Given these areas of uncertainty the manager must make the decision and implement it. A decision must be made even though the information is incomplete, even though not all the factors affecting the decision are known, and even though its ultimate impact cannot be ascertained. The manager must make the decision, implement it, control the action plan, and live with the consequences of that decision.

INVOLVING OTHER PEOPLE

To this point, the process of decision making has been described as if it were a solitary process involving only the manager. In reality most decisions involve the interaction of at least one person, and probably more, with the manager. The prudent manager will ensure that only decisions of minor importance are decided without consultation. Decisions of greater consequence, with results that will affect a number of people, will usually be discussed and analyzed with the manager's superior, colleagues, and frequently, subordinates. No individual can be the source of all knowledge, understanding, and analysis. In most cases, decision making is more effective if two or more people are involved. This does not mean the manager abdicates responsibility for making the decision but simply acknowledges that other people may have contributions that are of value. The manager and subordinates must understand that the final decision and the responsibility for its consequences rest with the manager.

The extent to which people other than the manager participate in the decision making process should depend upon the importance of the decision to be made. In general, the more important the decision, the more people should be involved in it. Let us examine five different levels of participation in the decision making process:

Level 1. The manager makes the decision alone, based solely on a personal analysis of the problem, understanding of the factors involved, and weighing of the considerations that will affect the decision.

Level 2. The manager involves the subordinates in the decision making process by having them provide information. Their role is limited to that of information suppliers. The manager still makes the decision but utilizes the data provided.

Level 3. The manager discusses the problem and the possible decision with subordinates individually. Suggestions are solicited on an individual basis and the manager then makes the decision based upon the individual input from the subordinates.

Level 4. The problem is shared, with the subordinates acting as a group, and the manager obtaining ideas, suggestions, comments, information, etc. from them. The manager then makes the decision that may or may not reflect the consensus of the group.

Level 5. The manager and subordinates work as a team to analyze the problem, develop alternative solutions, gather the data, consider the factors involved, and hopefully arrive at a consensus decision that is supported by all members of the group. While acting as moderator of the discussion, and with final responsibility for the decision, the manager does not impose his/her will upon the group and makes it known that in all likelihood the consensus of the group will be accepted.

WHICH TECHNIQUE SHOULD BE USED?

In considering these five levels of the decision making process it should not be thought that any one of them is more efficient or effective than any other. In fact, the proper process for any particular decision depends upon the problem being considered, the nature of the group involved, the leadership style of the manager, and a host of other factors. In general one can say that the five levels of decision making techniques should be applied to problems in ascending order of importance; in other words, Level 1 technique should be applied to problems of least importance and Level 5 applied to problems of greatest importance.

This is true if for no other reason than that the level of

acceptance of the decision, the effectiveness of its implementation, and the acknowledgment of its validity become increasingly greater as you move from Level 1 to Level 5. The more participation by the group in the decision making process itself, the greater their support and acceptance of the decision.

IMPLEMENTATION

Implementation is the last step in the decision making process. In making any decision a manager must develop an action plan, which considers how it is to be implemented, who is to do the implementation, and who will be affected by the implementation. One person must be put in charge of, and made responsible for, the action plan, although other people may be assigned to assist in its implementation.

The resources needed to accomplish the action plan should be carefully listed. These would include human, physical, or financial factors. A definite time limit should be established. If the action plan is detailed and extensive, it should be broken down into substeps with a time line established and dates set for the accomplishment of interim steps. A procedure for reporting progress should be established.

Last and perhaps most important, the process by which the decision is communicated to those affected by it should be clearly established. This process of communication is essential to the accomplishment of the objective. It is necessary that the communication of the decision be made down to the lowest level where the decision will have an impact. Finally, for the protection of all, and the clarity of procedures, the decision should be put in writing, along with the action plan and the procedure for monitoring the plan. Remember, the essential rule of business is, "If it isn't in writing, it never happened."

EXERCISES

Describe one decision that you are now, or soon will be, faced with.

What do you hope to accomplish by the decision?

What factors affect the decision?

What are the unknowns?

List three possible alternatives

    1.

    2.

    3.

Whom should you consult about the decision?

Who will be affected by this decision?

Whose support is needed to make the decision workable?

How will the decision be implemented?

    Who?

    Where?

    When?

    How?

NOTE

1. Alan M. Kantrow, "Why Read Peter Drucker?," *Harvard Business Review* (January-February 1980).

8PROBLEM FINDING

In the world of business, there is almost always one thing that follows on the heels of success—trouble. The buggy industry is wiped out by the automobile industry. Big American cars lose 20 percent of their market to foreign imports because of rising gasoline prices. Television networks watch in dismay as their viewers are won away by superstations, cable companies, video games, and home recorders. Polaroid spends hundreds of millions of dollars to develop a product, self-developing home movies, that apparently has no market. Xerox trades millions of shares of its stock for computer companies, publishers, *et al.*, and in the process causes its share price to fall by 75 percent. American steel companies pay out regular dividends instead of upgrading their obsolete physical plants and then cry for import duties on Japanese steel produced by modern, efficient mills. Real estate investment trusts operate with 98 percent borrowed money to get increased leverage and then go belly up when the prime rate hits 12 percent. RCA and Singer decide that their expertise in producing television sets and sewing machines qualifies them to enter the computer market and end up taking a combined loss of over half a billion dollars. Playboy Enterprises opens clubs and resorts all over the world and subsidizes their losses out of magazine profits.

Need I go on or do you get the picture? Even AT&T and IBM, probably the two best run companies in America, are beginning to feel the hot breath of serious competition. Why is it that success so often leads only to trouble? The ancient Greeks, with their keen understanding of human nature, help provide an answer.

Greek mythology is full of stories of persons raised to positions of power and wealth because the gods smiled upon them. Many times such persons came to believe that their eminence was due entirely to their own abilities and efforts, and failed to pay proper homage to the gods for their favor. The Greek word for this attitude is *hubris*, which is defined as ". . . arrogance resulting from excessive pride. . . ." Often the gods became offended by a person displaying hubris and would decide to punish that person. Rather than take direct action, the gods would ask Nemesis, the goddess of retributive justice, to prepare a suitable punishment. Nemesis would arrange the affairs of the errant mortal so that his arrogance would precipitate action that would lead to his downfall. (Richard Nixon and his staff are the most notable recent victims of hubris and its consequences.)

Hubris can also afflict corporations. In most of the examples cited above, companies got themselves into trouble because they believed that their success was due to their own extraordinary abilities, and that this success could be transferred to other fields, even though they might have had no expertise in those fields. Hubris can also lead to complacency. The movie industry, the automobile industry, and the steel industry all believed that they would never be touched by outside competition. Apparently the managers of television, foreign cars, and Japanese steel failed to accept the impossibility of competing against such impeccably managed enterprises.

A company that suffers from hubris is still solving the problems it encounters; unfortunately, it is not solving the problems it has not yet encountered. Arrogance prevents many successful companies from critically examining their marketplace, their products, or their procedures. Such companies operate on the unspoken assumption that their success will last forever and that any problems that arise will be easily handled. It is certain that even now Nemesis is planning a suitable punishment for such arrogant and complacent companies.

Norman Mackworth has stated that, "The distinction between the problem-solver and the problem-finder is critical."[1] As important as problem solving is, problem finding is sometimes more important. Problem finding is necessary if troubles are to be avoided, not just handled.

Managers need to be able not only to analyze data in financial statements and written reports, but also to scan the business environment for less concrete clues that a problem exists. They must be able to read meaning into changes in methods of doing business and into the actions of customers and competitors which may not show up in operating statements for months or even for years.

But the skill they need cannot be developed merely by analyzing problems discovered by someone else; rather, it must be acquired by observing first hand what is taking place in business. While the analytical skills needed for problem solving are important, more crucial to managerial success are the perceptual skills needed to identify problems long before evidence of them can be found by even the most advanced management information system. Since these perceptual skills are extremely difficult to develop in the classroom, they are now largely left to be developed on the job.[2]

All of this relates back to the questioning attitude that is so critical to the success of a manager. In order to find, or anticipate, problems it is necessary to question the basic tenets under which your unit is operating. Are you prepared for abrupt changes in personnel? What would you do if your two key subordinates suddenly left? As a sales manager, how are you going to control expenses when gas is $2.00 a gallon, a hotel room is $75.00 a night even outside New York, and a modest dinner costs $35.00? As an office manager, what are you going to do when, very shortly, none of your applicants has anything but the most rudimentary reading or math skills? As a warehouse manager, what are you going to do when the prime rate hits 20 percent and you are ordered to reduce inventory and increase efficiency? As a production manager, how will you maintain productivity when your employees demand a greater voice in determining work standards?

In every business there are trends or factors in the marketplace that will affect your unit. If you are to function at maximum efficiency you must anticipate the problems that are not yet upon you and seek some way to avoid or lessen them. Problem finding is an active rather than reactive process. It requires an understanding of your business, an awareness of matters that can affect your business, and the ability to extrapolate from limited data. A good start is to ask frequently, "What if . . .?" If you imagine the worst sequence of events you may often be right. If you imagine the most favorable sequence you will almost always be wrong.

To change the future one must first anticipate it.

NOTES

1. Norman H. Mackworth, "Originality," in *The Discovery of Talent*, ed. Dael Wolfle (Cambridge, Mass.: Harvard University Press, 1969).

2. J. Sterling Livingston, "Myth of the Well-Educated Manager," *Harvard Business Review* (January-February 1971).

9MOTIVATION

Just as problem solving and decision making are inextricably linked together, so motivation and leadership are joined like the strands of a double helix. A good leader is always a good motivator. In real life these two elements of managerial effectiveness cannot be separated. However, for purposes of study and clarification of the concepts and techniques involved, we will examine them separately so as to understand the essential elements of each. We will begin by examining motivation in this chapter and continue with a study of leadership in the next chapter.

A study of motivation must begin with a study of people, and of the assumptions that we as managers make about them. Until the first quarter of the twentieth century managers generally believed that people were inherently hostile to work. It was felt that people would avoid work whenever possible and only did it when forced to. This assumption led to the belief that people at work had to be controlled, directed, and threatened in order to get them to perform productively. There was also an underlying assumption that the working class preferred controls because they did not want to be in a position where they had to accept responsibility. Based on this set of assumptions, the way to increase productivity is to maximize control, direction, and fear.

In 1927, the Western Electric Company at their Hawthorne Works near Chicago undertook a study of worker productivity that seemed to refute the assumption that people disliked work and must be forced into it. The Hawthorne investigators did not set out to consider the impact of motivation on productivity; their initial purpose was to discover the effects of fatigue on the output of women assemblers. They began by separating a group of five women from the other assemblers, explaining to them the purpose of the research, and enlisting their cooperation. The investigators initiated a series of changes with the control group, involving number of rest periods, length of rest periods, variations in lunch time, lengthening and shortening of the work day, elimination of Saturday work, and various other changes. To the astonishment of the investigators each new change brought increased productivity. Productivity even increased when working time was shortened and Saturday work eliminated. Finally the investigators ended the experiments, returned the five women to their normal work stations, and watched in amazement as their productivity increased even more. By now the investigators were completely confused and interviewed the women involved to find what had caused the increases in productivity. They determined from their interviews that the women considered themselves a select group, helping the company solve a problem, and that the special attention made them feel important, gave them status, and provided a meaning and importance to their work that had not existed before. The conclusion of the investigators was that working conditions had less effect upon productivity than the attitude of the workers. The conclusion drawn was that by changing worker attitudes, productivity could also be changed.

The investigators also discovered that they had inadvertently done some things that were at variance from the way employees were normally treated by their supervisors. They had enlisted the cooperation of the employees in the study to be made and had consulted with them before changes were made. They held regular conferences with the women and solicited their reactions to the changes. They had enhanced team spirit by allowing the women to talk while working. And, finally, the investigators had made it known that the results of the various changes were important, and shared with the women the information on changes and output as it became available.

The Hawthorne studies prompted other investigators to analyze the relationship between productivity and the basic needs of workers. Out of these studies came the conclusion that not all people are motivated by the same factors, and that these differences must be understood by managers if they are to attain proper performance from their employees. One of the most significant of these studies was conducted at Texas Instrument Corporation in 1963. Their findings were that the factors most important in motivating an employee depended upon the kind of position the employee had. Among company scientists, the work itself and company policies were the most important factors in motivation. Among engineers, the primary factors were the opportunity for advancement, the assumption of responsibility, and the work itself. Manufacturing supervisors also placed the opportunity for advancement first among the factors that motivated them, with responsibility a close second. Technicians paid by the hour were primarily motivated by the opportunity to exercise responsibility, with advancement placing second. The principal motivating factor for hourly assemblers was the competence and friendliness of their supervisors.

These and other studies led Douglas McGregor to identify two separate sets of assumptions about why people work productively. According to McGregor, the two theories of management are Theory X and Theory Y. He labeled the traditional management assumption about people's dislike of work as Theory X and developed his own Theory Y as an alternative. According to McGregor, a Theory Y manager makes the following assumptions about people. First, people enjoy work and derive satisfaction from it. Second, people can effectively direct their own work activities if they are motivated toward a specific goal. Third, the average worker will not only accept, but actively seek, responsibility. And fourth, the capacity of most people is only partially utilized in the work they are doing. Theory X holds that people work because they have to and that it is the promise of increased pay or better benefits that motivates them to perform better. Theory Y says that people basically enjoy their work and can be made more productive by making the work more satisfying to them.

The problem that McGregor does not address is his assumption that everyone falls under Theory Y. It would seem that he is making the same mistake as a mill owner of the 1880s who assumed that all his people hated their work and had to be forced to do it. McGregor feels that everyone basically enjoys their work and need only to have it made more satisfying in order to increase productivity. Both the mill owner and McGregor lump people together into one category. For anyone who has exercised responsibility for the work of others it is obvious that both the mill owner and McGregor are correct. Some people do fall into the Theory X category. Every manager has experienced the frustration of attempting to get productive work out of an employee who seems to take little or no interest in the work, is content to do the very minimum required, and cannot wait to escape at the end of the day. Each manager has probably also worked with subordinates who found their work exciting and stimulating and attacked it with enthusiastic zest. What is frequently most puzzling is that many times these two people are doing the same task. It may be argued by McGregor that the unmotivated worker is simply in a job not suited to individual interests or abilities and that with proper placement that worker would be as motivated and productive as anyone. Therefore, it might be argued that everyone is a Theory Y worker when in the proper job. This may be true but is of little comfort to a manager who must direct the unit's operations with the people that are available.

Regardless of whether subordinates are Theory X people, Theory Y people, or as usual a mix of the two, the manager who is to perform effectively must do what is required to maximize productivity. A manager must drive the Theory X people with firmness and an insistence that production standards be met. They should understand that any deviation from acceptable standards will result in termination. The Theory Y worker must be motivated by public recognition, tasks with visible results, and occasional delegated responsibility.

In spite of the mix of subordinates there are specific procedures and techniques that can be used to motivate people. These techniques will not necessarily turn an uninterested, lethargic employee into a hard-charging dynamo but they will enable a manager to stimulate whatever self-motivation does exit. These are techniques that are employed by every capable manager and should represent the essential elements in the way that manager deals with subordinates.

The eight essential factors involved in motivation are:

—Self-Involvement

—Delegation

—Empathy

—Praise

—Blame

—Confidence

—Competence

—Fear

An effective manager and competent leader will use all these factors in dealing with subordinates. These factors should not be thought of as isolated elements but rather as parts of a whole. Each employee should probably be exposed to all these techniques over a period of time with the amount of exposure to any one factor varying from one employee to another. It is the manager's responsibility to understand and analyze subordinates and to know which factors are most effective with which individuals.

SELF-INVOLVEMENT

A manager must make work important to the people doing it. All of us work more effectively when we feel that the tasks we are performing are important, that others are depending upon us, and that we are doing something that we want to do rather than what someone else wants us to do. People also perform better when they are working at a task that they feel competent to perform. A wise manager will, whenever possible, assign people to jobs in which they feel competent and comfortable. When that is not possible the manager will ensure that an employee has adequate training and preparation, and is assigned proper supervision until the employee can function without day-to-day supervision.

In assigning an employee to a task, or responsibility for a project, the manager should discuss it in appropriate detail with the employee, soliciting suggestions and ideas and allowing full freedom of expression. This does not mean that the manager must in all cases accede to the wishes of the employee, but by letting the employee have his/her say the manager provides a basis for involving the employee in the acceptance of responsibility for the task.

Whenever possible the manager should plant the seeds for ideas or suggestions that might eventually come from the employee. It might take a day, a week, or a month before the idea comes back to the manager but when it does it will be the employee's own idea and he/she will be committed to its success. Sometimes it. is necessary to issue direct orders but many times, especially where time is not critical, it is more profitable for the manager to plant the seeds of future ideas, allow them to germinate, and then reap the benefits when the employee returns with specific suggestions.

None of us enjoys working in isolation where the results of our labor disappear into the void and we are left with no feeling of accomplishment. The effective manager lets a subordinate know the results of the work, or tasks, or responsibilities assigned. This type of feedback provides reinforcement about the value of an employee's work and position within the company. The results of work should be transmitted as soon as they are known so that the action-feedback-reinforcement loop is made as brief as possible. A person truly involved in work is vitally interested in the results of that work. A good manager will ensure that all subordinates are aware of the results of their efforts and the contribution they make toward achieving the objectives of the group.

DELEGATION

When surveyed about the shortcomings of managers, top executives place inability to delegate among the most critical of these shortcomings. Many a promising managerial career has stagnated over an inability to delegate responsibility properly. Managers who find it difficult to delegate are usually afraid of losing control of the task or the job involved. They fear that unless they do it themselves it will not be done properly. Such managers tend to be perfectionists, or overly cautious, or excessively concerned about the security of their own position. Regardless of the cause, an inability to delegate responsibility can quickly lead to a stalemated career.

The manager who does not delegate properly is losing a most valuable motivational tool. A manager who delegates work and responsibility gets people involved in their work. Delegation says that the manager has confidence in the employee and has faith that the task will be performed properly. It gives the employee an opportunity to exercise judgment and independent action, which are essential for growth. It provides a valuable learning experience and allows employees to feel that they are making significant contributions to the company.

The wise manager understands that *delegation does not mean abdication*. Authority to accomplish a task is delegated but not responsibility for that task. Therefore, the task that is delegated is not forgotten until the employee reports back. Whenever a task is delegated to a subordinate, an effective manager establishes a system to monitor the progress and performance of the employee in completing that task. As a wise manager once put it, "You inspect what you expect."

When a task is delegated to a subordinate it is the responsibility of the manager to make sure that the subordinate has been trained in the skills necessary to complete that task. The subordinate should develop a step-by-step road map of the route by which he/she expects to reach his/her destination. The manager should sign off on the action plan and then closely monitor the progress.

In delegating authority, the wise manager will describe the objective to be accomplished and then allow the subordinate to develop the procedure and methods for accomplishing that objective. The manager should clearly understand how the subordinate is going to go about the task and should not interfere unless it is apparent that the subordinate is wandering considerably off course. Sometimes when errors are not too detrimental it is helpful to allow the subordinate to correct his/her own mistakes. The subordinate should not feel that the manager is continually looking over his/her shoulder but should know that regular reports are expected to keep the manager fully apprised of the situation.

EMPATHY

In a modern industrial society it is important that employees feel they are more than just an employee number stored within a computer. They need to know that their manager has an interest in them as individuals, cares about them as persons, and is doing whatever is necessary to look out for their best interests. A manager who does not project a sincere interest in the well-being of subordinates will find it difficult to secure their cooperation on those occasions when the group is called upon for maximum effort. Or, as Machiavelli put it, "It is essential for a prince to be on a friendly footing with his people, since, otherwise, he will have no recourse in adversity."

The building of team spirit is an important requirement for any manager, and the ability to empathize with subordinates, and to take a sincere interest in them and their problems, is an essential element in building team spirit. In any business situation there is an inevitable parent-child relationship that exists between managers and subordinates. Just as children expect warmth, understanding, and concern for their welfare from parents, so subordinates expect those same qualities from a manager. A child that does not receive this emotional nourishment is likely to become recalcitrant and resentful. A manager who fails to provide emotional nourishment for subordinates is going to find a similar reaction.

It should be noted that a manager must walk that thin line between the interests of the company and the interests of the individual. The effective manager strives to maintain a balance between these two often conflicting interests. This is not an easy task but as long as subordinates feel that their manager cares about them and is being fair in representing the company position, they will in most cases give the manager the benefit of the doubt.

A manager must be careful not to slip into the position of becoming excessively involved in the personal affairs of employees. A manager must remember that the focus is on getting the job done. Whatever personal problems employees have should be left at home as much as possible. Sometimes these problems will impair the ability of the employee to work effectively and it is at those times that the manager must get involved, but only to the extent necessary to restore the employee to productive work habits. The manager is neither clergyman, physician, nor psychiatrist, and should not try to fill any of those roles.

The motivational value to be derived from a manager's sincere interest in subordinates is one that no manager should spurn. It can smooth many rough edges as a team works together toward a common goal.

PRAISE

Praise is a two-edged sword that cuts in both directions. It is a valuable tool for rewarding accomplishment and generating additional incentive but it can also be a source of resentment and insecurity. Anytime praise is given it is, in effect, an evaluation. Many people are made uncomfortable when they realize they are being, or have been, evaluated. It is this aspect of evaluation that makes certain people uncomfortable when they receive praise.

You will have noticed that many people will attempt to reject praise by saying, "Oh well, thanks, but it really wasn't that much." Many times a person will attempt to deflect the praise by mentioning others who contributed to the project. These reactions may be manifestations of false modesty but often they are indications that the person is genuinely uncomfortable when faced with praise.

Most of us, too, are by now quite wary of praise. We have all worked for managers who prefaced every criticism with a bit of insincere praise. Managers who began with, "John, you have really been doing fine work, *but* I'd like to talk to you about. . . ." We have all come to fear that, "but . . .". A wise manager does not dissipate the value of praise by using it as a prelude to criticism.

For praise to have maximum impact, it should be used sparingly, not at every opportunity. It should not be distributed like the largesse of French kings who threw coins to the peasants while passing through the streets of Paris. Indiscriminate, excessive praise serves no purpose and can have a harmful effect upon an employee. Excessive use will debase the coin of praise and render it valueless. When that happens praise loses all its worth as a motivating factor.

The wise manager selects the occasions on which to praise a subordinate. The accomplishment to be praised should not be part of the routine work of the subordinate but represent exceptional and outstanding performance. In addition, the praise should not be general but specific. For instance, "That report you submitted for inclusion in next year's operating plan was first-rate. I was especially impressed with the market research that you did on the demographics for women's magazines. Your analysis of the market trends was both concise and convincing and was a big help to me." That type of praise is far more productive and motivating than the usual, "Charlie, that was a terrific report that you turned in and I'm really proud of you boy. Keep up the good work." Moliere's view was that, "Simple praise does not put a man at his ease; there must be something solid mixed with it."

A good manager will avoid the issuance of excessive praise, and thereby avoid being considered either a fool or a hypocrite by subordinates. Praise should be issued sparingly, specifically, and only when it is truly merited by outstanding performance. The infrequency of praise will render it all the more valuable and create in the employees a desire to earn it.

BLAME

All employees are entitled to the security of knowing where they stand with their managers. If something was done wrong, the employee is entitled to know it and to receive direction on how to avoid making a similar mistake in the future. The assignment of blame is an essential part of a manager's responsibility but one that in certain areas of business almost seems to have disappeared. If a mistake has been made, then the employee probably knows it and is psychologically expecting to be reprimanded. The reprimand should be administered in a dispassionate, objective way with corrective measures included. The employee will be grateful and will simultaneously experience relief from the guilt feelings that were engendered by the mistake. Managers who do not correct mistakes of subordinates seriously undermine their own authority. If a mistake occurs and a manager does not institute corrective procedures, then the employee must assume that the manager has no interest in the work that is being performed, or is too ignorant to be able to detect error. The end result is a loss of respect for the manager and a gradual disappearance of the manager's effective authority.

Pardon one offense and you encourage the commission of many.—Publicus Syrus

An effective manager will demand the best from subordinates and will set standards high enough so that acceptable performance is really outstanding performance. These standards must be clearly communicated to the subordinates and when anyone falls short, the manager must immediately correct the shortcoming and institute a corrective plan of action. This aspect of managerial responsibility is so critical to group performance that it will be considered separately in Chapter 13, The Pygmalion Effect.

CONFIDENCE

The good manager and the outstanding leader radiate confidence. They always give the impression that they are on top of their job, that they know what they are doing, and that no matter what problems occur they are capable of handling them. All strong managers are overtly confident. Regardless of their inner feelings their external appearance is always one of calm assurance. A confident, assured manager gives subordinates a feeling of security. They feel that under strong leadership their unit will prosper and their manager has strength to fight for them and their interests should the need arise. The confidence that a manager shows will be transmitted to subordinates, as can other traits. If a manager is nervous, insecure, and easily rattled, then it won't be long before the subordinates are evidencing much the same characteristics. Conversely the confident, assured, and determined manager will transmit those characteristics to subordinates.

COMPETENCE

All of us want to work for somebody who really knows the job, someone who has a real understanding of the operations of the company, and who has established specific goals for the unit. The competence that such a manager demonstrates provides essential security to subordinates. They know that they are being led in the proper direction and in the most efficient, productive manner. A subordinate working for such a manager expects to learn from that manager. A competent manager will be eager to share understanding and knowledge. The guidance that subordinates need to further develop their skills will be provided. A manager should be constantly studying, learning, and analyzing in order to develop increased competency. A competent manager is not standing still but is looking forward and moving forward, constantly learning more and more about the job, the business, and the industry. Competence cannot easily be faked, and the level of competence by a manager will be quickly ascertained by subordinates. If as a manager you do not feel that you have a complete grasp of your job, then you should be doing everything you can to increase your understanding and skills.

FEAR

Modern social theory tends to downplay the importance of fear as a motivating influence in the business world. When fear is discussed, it is usually described as a negative factor. In theory, and in the classroom, this view may have some validity. In the real world of business, fear is an essential element of motivation. It should, however, be made clear that the type of fear that is desirable is not terror. Subordinates who are so terrorized that they are unable to function independently are of little use to anyone. What is desirable is a certain amount of apprehension, which will arise from knowing that when mistakes are made, they will be immediately detected and the guilty party will have to answer for them.

The moderate apprehension that subordinates should feel is a measure of their respect for the manager. They respect a manager's opinion of them and their work and they fear disapproval. The subordinates of an effective manager know that standards are high and that everyone is expected to meet those standards. Subordinates should be apprehensive of their ability to match the standards of their manager. Because of their respect for the manager and their need for approval they will strive as hard as they can to meet those standards.

SUMMARY

As a manager you should be aware of the eight factors that affect the motivation of the people who report to you. The way you employ these eight factors and the degree to which each one is employed is a matter of your own managerial style and leadership skills. It should also depend to a certain extent upon the individual that you are dealing with. The important thing is that each one of these factors be understood and that you as a manager know when, where, and how to apply them.

A FINAL NOTE

We have talked earlier about how a manager must use the resources of time and energy efficiently. If you are presently trying to motivate an employee who has the ability to do the job properly but is failing because of apathy and indifference, give it up. In my years in business I have never seen an indifferent employee turned into an achiever without changing jobs. Do not waste your time on that isolated individual who has little or no interest in his/her work. Get rid of that person. Devote your time and energy to the bulk of your subordinates who are performing reasonably well but who could do better if properly motivated. This group will respond to your efforts and will provide a good return on the investment of your resources.

EXERCISES

Describe briefly one situation in which you were involved, or one that you observed, where an employee was successfully motivated by a manager.

Describe the employee:

Describe the manager:

Describe the procedures used by the manager:

Describe the outcome:

10LEADERSHIP

*Every great leader has the ability to
inspire his followers to share a
common vision.*—Peter Drucker

I have got good news and bad news. The bad news is that most of
the problems you will encounter as a manager are probably not
solvable by the process described in previous chapters. This is
because most of your problems will involve people—people who
won't work together, people who are in the wrong job, people who
have little or no interest in their work, people with family or
personal problems, people who are content to get by with minimum
effort, and a host of other problems associated with the fact that
humans are a very imperfect species.

The good news is that a capable manager can learn how to deal
with a multitude of people-related problems and weld together an
effective working team. Some of the most satisfying moments in a
manager's career come from watching a team of subordinates
perform well in a trying situation. The manager knows that
without proper leadership and guidance the team would be ineffective, wasting its energy and time in personal conflicts or apathetic
attitudes.

The starting point in dealing successfully with people problems
is proper leadership from the manager, and the respect that will
ensue. Leadership creates an air of authority so that people can
focus on goals and not waste time in back-biting or second-

guessing. Fortunately, any intelligent person with diligence and effort can become an effective leader. The first step is to understand the characteristics of a successful leader. The second step is to consciously develop leadership skills. The third step is to practice and apply the techniques of good leadership.

In trying to analyze and describe leadership, social scientists and management researchers have a tendency to get very abstract. Abstractions may be useful in defining the concept of leadership but are of little help to a manager seeking guidance. If nothing else, managers are pragmatic and want to know what works. Fortunately, there are certain characteristics of leadership that have been identified. Obviously not every leader shares all these characteristics to the same extent and many leaders lack some of them entirely. However, in such cases the leader possesses one or more other characteristics in abundance to make up for the elements that are lacking.

Among the necessary elements for effective leadership are:

—*Enthusiasm.* Not the manic enthusiasm of a cheerleader but the quiet, focused energy of the person who knows where to go and exactly how to get there. The leader's enthusiasm manifests itself in obvious pleasure in the work to be done and the high energy level brought to it. The effective leader is enthusiastic because he/she enjoys work and considers it to be of importance. This feeling is transmitted to subordinates by example and attitude. There is no way in which a manager can extract optimum performance from subordinates when transmitting a feeling that the work is of little importance. If a manager's attitude indicates that the work is a daily chore that must be gotten through, then it is impossible to transmit enthusiasm to subordinates and to inspire them to share a common vision.

—*Confidence.* George Herbert once said that "Skill and confidence are an unconquered army." A leader is confident, and is able to make decisions and accept the consequences of those decisions. A leader's optimism is not based upon wishful thinking but on a sound assessment of his/her capabilities and those of subordinates. A confident leader does not deny the possibility of error but learns from mistakes and ensures that they will not be repeated. However, the possibility of error is never allowed to be an excuse for inaction. The confident leader's motto might be characterized as, "Sometimes wrong but never in doubt."

—*Integrity.* A leader is dependable. Subordinates know that they can rely upon their leader to honor all commitments, large or small. A leader with integrity does not base actions on self-interest or treat subordinates with favoritism. The basic integrity of a good leader provides the kind of courage that is necessary to stand up for the rights of subordinates. That courage also enables a manager to pursue a course known to be correct even though he/she may suffer the disapproval of colleagues in doing so.

—*Intelligence.* A leader who is stupid is a contradiction in terms. There is a minimum level of intelligence required for leadership that is such that most of the population can qualify to be leaders. The important factor is not how much intelligence a leader has but how that intelligence is used. The mind of a leader should be open, questioning, and receptive to new ideas and experiences.

—*Competence.* The untried rookie does not manage the major league baseball team; the recent accounting graduate is not put in charge of the finance department. With experience should come the competence that earns a leader the respect of subordinates, and these two factors provide the credibility that allows that leader to function effectively.

The attentive reader will have noted the similarity between the characteristics of leadership and those factors that a manager needs in order to properly motivate people. There is only one way that a leader can inspire people to share a common vision and that is by motivating them. Leadership is the source from which motivation develops.

The knowledgeable reader will also have noticed the omission of one characteristic of leadership that is frequently identified by academicians, consultants, and other theoreticians. This characteristic is usually described as friendliness, or warmth, or involvement with others. In a society based upon egalitarianism it is not surprising that many social scientists would seek to insert those values into situations where they are inappropriate. The facts may dismay sociologists but it is not necessary that a leader exhibit feelings of warmth or humanitarianism. The roster of outstanding leaders is filled with austere and detached figures. One need only think of Charles deGaulle, Woodrow Wilson, and John D. Rockefeller to realize that warmth and friendliness are not essential characteristics of a leader.

All outstanding leaders do share one characteristic. They are perceived by their followers, and others, to be winners. They give the impression that whatever they undertake will be successful. People want to be associated with a winner and eagerly join with the person who offers the promise of success. In some cases this promise becomes a self-fulfilling prophecy. If enough people believe that something will happen, then their actions, and the response of others to their certainty, ensure the success that was anticipated.

Aside from the personal characteristics that most leaders share there is also the key question of how a leader functions effectively. Leaders function effectively by doing pretty much what any effective manager is expected to do:

1. Set clear objectives.

2. Organize and plan the manner in which the objectives will be attained.

3. Enlist the cooperation and support of subordinates.

4. Demand high standards of performance from subordinates.

5. Objectively analyze problems and make sound decisions based upon that analysis.

6. Select proficient subordinates and provide the training they require to work effectively.

Of these six functions of a leader, numbers three through six are considered in separate chapters. Numbers one and two are touched upon in a number of different chapters but a more detailed discussion is warranted here.

SET CLEAR OBJECTIVES

Every group looks to its leader for direction; members of a group want and need to be told where they are going. They expect the leader to have the necessary information not available to the group and to decide upon their objectives. Group members regard this as a necessary function of leadership and resent an attempt to transfer this responsibility to the group. A wise leader is not misled by erroneously applied principles of democratic procedure into avoiding the responsibility for setting group goals. The leader must set goals in a clear and confident manner. *First Corinthians* states,

"For if the trumpet give an uncertain sound, who shall prepare himself to the battle?" Every group is entitled to hear their leader's trumpet, clearly and forcefully. Where are you taking your people? If you know, let them know. If you're not sure, make certain of your goal and then let them know.

If a manager does not have a set of objectives clearly in mind, then his/her manager is also at fault. It is not enough to accept that situation and wait for a higher authority to issue instructions. The motivated manager will prepare a list of objectives and take them to his/her manager for approval. This forces a consideration by both parties and an eventual agreement. It is not possible for a manager to function effectively without specific objectives. The warning of Seneca should be heeded, "When a man does not know what harbor he is making for, no wind is the right wind."

Once objectives are set and clearly transmitted to the group, a plan to accomplish them must be developed. It is at this point that group participation can be useful. The destination has been decided upon and now the best route can be discussed. The manager may regard this as a decision to be analyzed according to the principles outlined in Chapter 7, Decision Making. The leadership style of each manager will determine how much group participation is permitted.

Refer to the five levels of participation in Chapter 7. The prudent manager knows that to win the cooperation and support of subordinates they should be allowed a voice in the development of the working plan. During the discussion the leader should not dominate the meetings. His role should be one of encouraging full discussion and stimulation of ideas. His manner is, perhaps, best described by Tacitus, "Reason and calm judgement, the qualities specially belonging to a leader."

ORGANIZE AND PLAN WHAT IS TO BE DONE

An effective work plan to accomplish group objectives provides:

- An efficient use of the resources of people, money, equipment, and time.
- Interim checkpoints that serve as signals of potential problems.
- Each worker with a clear understanding of what is expected.
- Built-in controls to monitor the efficiency and quality of work.

- A timetable that provides coordination of individual projects.

- Clear responsibility for all significant aspects of the plan.

- Contingency plans to accommodate possible problems.

DON'T NEGLECT DETAILS

There is one additional function of the effective manager. While setting goals, motivating people, and planning ahead, the prudent manager must also watch the details. It is possible for a manager to be preoccupied with big issues and be tripped up by small details. A lack of attention to details can spoil the most carefully thought out operating plan. The wise manager knows what each subordinate is doing at all times. All subordinates should know that at any moment they are liable to be asked about their work. The manager's questions should be specific, reaching down to the finest detail of the subordinate's work. The manager should also take this opportunity to solicit suggestions on how the work could be done easier, better, faster, or cheaper.

Slight not what's near, through aiming at what's far.— Euripides

Constant probing of this type serves a number of purposes:

- It keeps the manager totally informed about activities, problems, and attitudes within the department.

- It generates useful ideas.

- It prevents sloppiness from creeping into the work because of inattention by the manager.

- It spotlights problems before they become major crises.

- It maintains the authority, and enforces the discipline, of the manager.

- It prevents surprises.

SOURCE OF POWER

Perceptive managers realize that their influence arises from a number of sources. In general, the more sources of power available to draw upon the stronger the manager's position will be. The principal sources of a leader's power are:

—*Legitimate.* The office conveys the power. Your official position by itself provides much of your authority. For new managers this may be all they can call upon until they become better known to the workers.

—*Monetary.* You have the power to grant, withhold, or determine the amount of pay increases.

—*Skill or Expertise.* If your competence is acknowledged by the group, then your decisions are far less apt to be questioned.

—*Affection.* If your people like you, they will be more willing to go along with you. However, a leader on a losing streak will soon find that the affection of subordinates is as lasting as a snow flake in spring.

—*Respect.* If you can't be loved, you can certainly be respected. Respect is earned by a manager who is dedicated, demanding, and fair. You will also find that respect will last though affection may fade.

—*Fear.* You have the power to hire and fire, and to promote or hold back. This power is most effective when implied. A leader using this power directly is demonstrating an inability to exercise leadership in other more productive ways.

BASIC RULES

There are certain basic rules of leadership. Each manager should know them and strive to follow them.

- Set a personal example.
- Strive for respect.
- Let affection develop without pursuing it.
- Give help to your people.
- Ask your people for advice and assistance.
- Develop a sense of responsibility in your people.

- Criticize behavior constructively.
- Treat your people as individuals.

Do but set the example yourself and I will follow you.—
Aesop

EXERCISES

Rate yourself on the characteristics of a leader. Use a scale from 1 (poor) to 10 (outstanding).

Personal	*Rating*
1. Enthusiasm	_____
2. Confidence	_____
3. Integrity	_____
4. Intelligence	_____
5. Competence	_____

Skills	
1. Setting objectives	_____
2. Organizing and planning	_____
3. Enlisting cooperation	_____
4. Setting high standards	_____
5. Problem analysis	_____
6. Decision making	_____
7. Recruiting	_____

Analyze the present sources of your power. Assign a percentage to each source showing its influence at this time.

Source	*% Of Influence*
Legitimate	_____
Monetary	_____
Skill or Expertise	_____
Affection	_____
Respect	_____
Fear	_____
Total	100%

List those areas of leadership characteristics and sources of power that are of concern to you.

Areas of Concern

1.

2.

3.

4.

11ORAL COMMUNICATION

In business most communication is done orally. We spend far more
time talking to one another than writing. Writing forces us to
organize our thoughts, and compels us to brevity. This constraint is
not applicable to speech. We can all talk for hours if so compelled
and need pay no respect to order or clarity of expression. Courtesy
on the part of our listeners (victims?) usually prevents them from
stopping our flow of words. Most people wait patiently for us to
wind down so they might interject a word or two.

An exaggeration, you say? Of course, but it does dramatize the
fact that few of us are as careful with our speech as we are with our
writing. And yet, whatever impression we make on other people is
largely based on what they hear us say. We are hired for a job by
talking with someone and convincing that person that we have the
ability to do the job. If we receive a promotion, it is because we
convinced someone that we can communicate effectively with our
new subordinates.

People judge us by what we say and what we do. Our mental
capacity, creativity, and potential are inferred from what we say
and how we say it. Can you express yourself with force and clarity?
Do your words express ideas that are organized, sequential, and
relevant to the discussion? Can you present your ideas with brevity

and preciseness? Consciously or not, as we deal with people they are making evaluations about us. Our ability is measured by what we say, not just by what we do.

A recent magazine article quotes a personnel manager, "I don't want to see anyone. Just let me listen to a man or woman for about two minutes and I'll tell you how promotable that person is."[1] That remark overstates the case but there is no question that significant promotions go to those with superior oral expression. Technical skills and the ability to handle people are also necessary for promotion. Yet all of us know many persons of great technical competence who have never been promoted, usually because their ability to deal with people is so poor. We also know many others with very high personal relations skills who have never moved above a first level of management. Their inability to express their thoughts with clarity and precision precludes them from rising higher in management.

Top managers in business usually pride themselves on their efficiency and that of their subordinates. It is embarrassing for a company president to have a vice president whose speech patterns are unfocused and discursive. Busy executives do not have time or patience to wait while someone wanders all around a topic before coming to a conclusion. After sitting through far too many business meetings, I can report that the most common phrases are, "Get to the point," "What are you driving at?," and the newest and most popular, "What's the bottom line?" No top manager will long tolerate a subordinate manager who misuses everyone's time with long-winded, disconnected discourses. That sort of embarrassment is usually alleviated by the quick transfer, demotion, or termination of the subordinate.

There are apparently four basic causes for an inability to speak with precision and brevity: A muddled, incoherent thought pattern; a stream-of-consciousness habit in speaking; an excessive fear of giving offense; and an attempt to avoid responsibility. We need not concern ourselves with the first cause because anyone with muddled and incoherent thought patterns has no future in business (politics would seem a far more suitable vocation).

As to the second cause, I know a young manager who is afflicted with logorrhea—saying too much about too little. He is very bright and when he talks each idea seems to spark two more. Each new idea is expressed as soon as it pops into his head, one idea after another tumbling forth with no coherence or sequential development. Stream-of-consciousness speech may be useful to a disturbed person in a therapeutic session with an analyst but it has no place in business. No one in business has the time or inclination to separate the wheat from the chaff of someone else's speech. Good ideas are not enough. They must be presented in minimum time with maximum persuasion. This requires clarity, coherence, and sequence in presentation. I fear for my young friend, for unless he learns to express himself more effectively he will never rise above his present position. All his intelligence, skill, and rapport with his co-workers will avail him little.

In our discussion of motivation you will recall the Theory X manager who drove his subordinates by using control and fear. There may have been a lot wrong with that manager but one thing he did properly was to talk straight to his subordinates. He was not concerned about possibly giving offense when he spoke to a subordinate, his primary thought was to direct the behavior of the subordinate as quickly and effectively as possible. His directions were brief and specific, and if they were too blunt so much the better. Whatever faults he may have had as a manager, at least his people had no doubt what was expected of them. Aside from the construction industry it is hard to think of a sector of American business where straight talk still prevails. We no longer have Theory X managers or even Theory Y; what we see today are Theory M managers—M for Mush. A Theory M manager's directions are phrased so obliquely and delicately to avoid giving offense that they have no more substance than a bowl of mush. No one is quite sure what a Theory M manager wants. Subordinates spend much time puzzling over their latest convoluted instructions, ringed with concentric circles of qualifying phrases. An example from *A Manager's Garden of Mushy Directions*:

> Oh, by the way Charlie, I was talking with the Big Boss the other day and one of the things that came up—incidentally he had some awfully good things to say about your work—anyway, one of the things that we were kicking around was this whole trend in our society where people just don't pay their bills anymore. I don't know what the problem is because when I was growing up it was a mortal sin not to pay your bills on time; I guess things have changed but I still can't get used to it. Anyhow, this whole thing is really getting sticky and it looks as if it may be causing us a wee bit of a problem. Before things start to get warm maybe we ought to take a look at all this and see what we come up with. I hate to ask you to put out anymore because you've done one hell of a job as manager of credit and collections and no one could be happier than I am at the way you've taken charge here and really shaped things up. Anyway, the Big Boss is getting a bit nervous

and I was wondering if you would have a chance to look at our aging schedule and give me your thoughts on where we stand. The only reason I bother you with this is that the Big Boss got a look at the last printout and noticed something about our receivables equalling five more Days of Sales than last year at this time. Before the boss gets too stirred up I'd like to give him something to calm him down. Would you help me out on this, Charlie, I'd really appreciate it.

Lest anyone think this example is exaggerated for effect, I assure you it is not. In fact compared to some manager's directions that I have heard, it might stand as a model of brevity and precision.

What the manager could have said is:

Charlie, our collections are starting to slow down. Receivables now equal 65 Days of Sales compared with 60 at this time last year. I want you to examine this problem and submit a written report to me by Friday, the 21st. I want you to identify the causes of this problem and recommend a series of steps to correct the problem.

Charlie may not care for this assignment but at least he knows what is expected of him. The problem was succinctly described for Charlie and he was clearly told what he must do about it and given a date for completion of the assignment.

I submit that we have become so sensitive to the feelings of others that we are losing the ability to speak clearly. People are not so hypersensitive that they cannot be given clear directions. In fact, people welcome receiving their assignments in the most unambiguous manner possible. Most workers do not want to decipher a five minute monologue to find what is expected of them. People do not take offense when someone talks straight to them. What is objectionable is the unspoken message, "I can't talk straight to you because you are too immature and sensitive to handle it." As a manager you should deal with superiors and subordinates alike; show respect for them by talking straight and treating them as adults.

The desire to avoid responsibility is the fourth cause of imprecise speech. This is the oral form of waffling that is discussed in Chapter 12, Written Communication. The essence of management is the desire not just to accept responsibility but to actively seek it. In any well managed company, wafflers will not be promoted. They may be tolerated in noncritical positions but they will never rise to levels where decisions are made. A good litmus test for the management strength of a company is to examine the prevailing speech patterns. Clear, direct, concise speech is almost always a sign of strong, capable management. Examine your own company. If you find the prevailing speech pattern is vague, rambling, and incoherent, you should give serious thought to moving to another company where strength and clarity of speech are considered virtues.

Guidelines For Better Communication

To develop better speech habits, the following recommendations are submitted:

- *Think and then speak*
  Don't always be the first to begin a discussion. Don't permit your initial thoughts to come pouring out in a stream of consciousness. Take a pause before speaking and edit your thoughts. As a child you may have had to blurt things out to get attention but that is a poor habit to carry into adulthood. A pause before speaking will also lend weight to your words.

- *Organize your thoughts*
  Good ideas by themselves are not enough. They must be expressed with clarity and precision. Edit your speech to remove verbosity, redundancy, waffling, and bloating just as you would in a written report. The sentences you speak should be as well ordered as those you write, but made more compelling by the force of your personality.

- *Be brief*
  This rule is always pertinent but especially when meeting with your superiors. Most managers do not have time for long, discursive soliloquies by their subordinates. Remember, you are only one of many persons seen by that manager in a day. Have consideration for his/her time and workload; make your reports brief and to the point. Respond to questions in the same manner and exit promptly when the discussion has obviously come to an end. Resist the tendency to bask in the warm glow of the boss's presence.

- *Focus on the main issues*
  In any discussion try to isolate the main issue and focus your attention upon it. Do not allow yourself or the discussion to be sidetracked onto peripheral matters. If matters of substance

arise, not pertinent to the main issue, they should be set aside to be analyzed at future meetings.

FORMAL PRESENTATION

A formal presentation is an opportunity for a manager to demonstrate competence, sometimes before peers, many times in front of superiors. A formal presentation is designed to transfer information from the speaker to the audience. It is also an occasion during which the person making the presentation will be judged on knowledge and competency. A manager assigned to a formal presentation should prepare thoroughly to ensure that maximum information is imparted and that one's competence and knowledge receive high marks. Thorough preparation will also provide the confidence necessary to control whatever nervousness the manager might feel.

Guidelines For Formal Presentations

- *Don't memorize*
  Unless you are an extraordinary performer, a memorized speech will be stiff and boring. In addition, a momentary loss of memory can be disastrous.

- *Don't read*
  Richard Burton may be able to read from a script and hold his audience's attention but few of us have that skill. Reading also prevents you from establishing contact with your audience and sensing their response to your presentation.

- *Use notes*
  Key words or phrases should be on cards for easy reference. Do not try to put the data for your presentation in notes, which notes should serve only as memory joggers. The cards should be inconspicuous and the printing should be large enough to be easily read.

- *Use visuals*
  People remember best what is heard *and* seen. Visuals are by themselves memory joggers and eliminate the necessity for much of your notes.

- *Memorize opening and close*
  A good speaker starts strong and finishes strong. You should

know exactly how you are going to begin and end. The beginning should preview the presentation and the ending should summarize and draw conclusions.

- *Use handouts carefully*
  Do not distribute handouts at the beginning of your talk. They should be distributed as you want them studied. Otherwise your audience will be reading while you are talking.

- *Fit your talk to your time*
  Do not take more time than is allotted to you. If you do not feel you have sufficient time to cover your assigned subject, ask for either more time or a more narrowly defined topic.

- *Rehearse*
  Use a tape recorder to record your presentation. Listen objectively and analyze the presentation according to your objectives. Revise your presentation aiming for clarity and precision. A timer should be used to keep within the allotted time.

Podium Skills

- *Never apologize*
  Accept the situation as given and make your presentation. Do not refer to your nervousness. Speakers who do so are trying to enlist the sympathy of the audience.

- *Do not use prepared jokes*
  Telling a joke successfully is a very rare skill, so rare that people who can do so earn handsome incomes as entertainers. If you want to open on a lighter note use a story from your own experience, but it should illustrate a point you wish to make.

- *Gesture naturally*
  Relax and let your own interest and enthusiasm direct your gestures. Do not think about your gestures or they will be stiff and forced.

- *Read your audience*
  Is your message coming across? Pay attention to the audience so you can gauge their reaction.

- *Keep your focus*
  Concentrate on two things, your audience and your message. Forget about yourself and think only about what you want to say and how it is being received.

- *Be yourself*
  Let your personality come through. Make your talk interesting by putting yourself into it. Relax, enjoy yourself, and give your audience a chance to do likewise.

  Speech is a mirror of the soul, as a man speaks, so is he.— Publicus Syrus

NOTE

1. Phyllis Martin, "What's In A Word Or Did I Say That?," *Aloft* (March 1980).

12 WRITTEN COMMUNICATION

Effective written communication is a skill essential to a manager. Almost all managers are required to write memos, proposals, reports, operating plans, etc. Much of this writing is intended for managers at higher levels and it provides superiors with insight into how the manager's mind works. Is there a clear grasp of problems? Is the material organized in an analytical, objective, sequential manner? Are the thought processes direct and orderly? Are ideas expressed concisely and forcefully? In short, is this the kind of person capable of assuming a position of greater responsibility?

Written communication is a reflection of the way a person's mind operates. There are few managers who have achieved significant success without the ability to write with precision and clarity. Their writings give evidence of knowing exactly what needs to be done and precisely how to do it. Every manager can benefit by paying closer attention to written communication. The wise manager strives for clarity, conciseness, and persuasiveness in writing.

Of all those arts in which the wise excel, Nature's chief masterpiece is writing well.—John Sheffield

There are certain basic questions that must precede writing:

- Whom am I writing for?
- What am I trying to accomplish?
- Do I have all the data?
- Are the data assembled in a logical, sequential order?

The answers to these questions provide writers with a clear picture of their audience, a clarification of their purpose, a collection of the necessary data, and an outline of what is to be written. It is only after these steps have been accomplished that the actual writing should begin. It is also at this point that the manager is faced with the problem of communicating with maximum clarity and understanding. The manager must develop a style that is simple, direct, and forceful; a style that leads sequentially from one point to another, with conclusions that are fully supported by the evidence. This is not as simple as it sounds. It requires that the data be assembled in sequence so that the relationship of each part to the whole can easily be seen. It requires logical transitions, so that each step proceeds inevitably to the next. It requires a careful selection of wording, so that the exact meaning of each sentence and paragraph is clearly seen. It requires that the writer avoid vague, ambiguous, and redundant phrasing so that uncertainty does not occur.

Fortunately all these requirements can be met by following basic principles of written expression. These principles are well established, easily identified, and quickly learned if they are practiced faithfully. Once learned they do not force everyone to write the same; rather, they liberate each writer to achieve maximum clarity and understanding while demonstrating individuality and a personal style.

To develop a clear, powerful writing style the effective manager should:

1. *Be concise*
2. *Be precise*
3. *Use familiar words*
4. *Use strong verbs*

BE CONCISE

One of the skills of an accomplished writer is to be clear and to be brief. Much of rewriting consists of removing excess words. A persuasive written communication is uncluttered. You must prune your sentences so the reader can know their meaning. There are four principal causes of excessive wordage: redundancy, verbosity, waffling, and bloating.

Redundancy is the unnecessary repetition of an idea; in some hands this has been raised to an art form. Some examples of redundancy are given below with corrections. Where a correction is not given fill in the blank with your own improvement.

Redundancy	*Correction*
The month of July	July
Large in size	Large
Any and all	———
Green in color	———
Consensus of opinion	———
Thirty-six pounds of weight	———
Adequate enough	———
Enclosed herewith	———
Few in number	———
Necessary requisite	———

Those who are unable to resist redundancies produce sentences such as "Each and every man and woman still continues as a general rule to use the consensus of opinion of their neighbors as a substitute for their own personal thoughts and ideas."

Those who resist the siren call of redundancy may still come to grief upon the hidden reef of *verbosity*—excessive use of verbs and prepositions. The result is stilted and overly formal phrasing. Prolonged exposure produces in the reader a heavylidded languor that can only be banished by cold draughts of clear, crisp prose.

Overweight Phrases

During the time that	<u>when</u>
Due to the fact that	<u>because</u>
In regard to	<u>about</u>
In the event that	————
At this point in time	————
At that point in time	————
Subsequent to	————
By means of	————
As to whether	————
Off of	————
In accordance with	————

Extra verbiage should not be allowed to creep into your sentences. Examine your phrasing as you do your waistline and keep each lean and fit.

Waffling reaches its highest level of perfection within government agencies. Unfortunately, it has also become widespread in business. The bite of the waffle bug renders people incapable of writing a simple, declarative statement. Examples and corrections follow.

Waffle Statement	*Translation*
In my judgment this proposal seems to have merit.	It's a good idea.
It appears that our efforts did not produce the anticipated eventuality.	It didn't work.
It seems likely that the response of our female personnel will be essentially negative.	The women won't like it.

Our view is consistent with that expressed by the print media.	We agree with the newspapers.
At this time it seems likely that our shortfall in anticipated revenues will result in a negative cash flow.	We're going broke.

Compose your own waffle statement in the space below. The winning entry will earn its author a choice of any GS-18 position within the federal Civil Service.

Bloating is an effort to make simple statements sound important. It produces sentences that appear to have significance beyond that of the subject. What is actually produced is an increase in the Gross National Prolixity (GNP).

Bloatings	*Simpler*
It is certain that the shipment will be made on time.	The shipment will be made on time.
In essence there are but three essential parts to the program.	The program has three parts.
In relation to expectations, it is self-evident that the marketing program has not achieved the success that was anticipated for it.	We missed our sales goal.
There were fourteen sales reps who made quota last year.	Fourteen sales reps made quota last year.
It is my plan to review all operating budgets.	I will review all operating budgets.

To avoid bloating your sentences be careful of *it* and *there*; they creep into a sentence, adding only to its length but not its clarity. Beware of constructions such as *there are . . ., there is . . ., it is . . .,* and *it is . . . that.*

Conciseness can be achieved by careful pruning of the evil weeds of redundancy, verbosity, waffling, and bloating. Do not allow your garden to be overrun by worthless undergrowth that obscures your ideas. (The careful writer should also be sparing in the use of metaphors, but that is another subject.)

BE PRECISE

It is possible to be brief and still be unclear. To wit, Ron Ziegler's classic remark after being caught in a lie, "That statement is now inoperative." It is brief, forceful, and totally uninformative. Precision in writing requires more than brevity. Precision is exactness—using the precise word or phrase to convey the intended meaning. Preciseness demands that a writer know the exact meanings of words used. Many words can be chosen to express a particular idea but usually only one word conveys the true meaning the writer intends.

An effective writer does not settle for the first word that comes to mind but finds the exact word to transmit the exact meaning. One would not use *halt* when one means *stop. Halt* is a temporary ending whereas *stop* implies a more permanent cessation. (Perhaps if we can persuade the highway authorities to change their STOP signs to HALT signs we can begin using the words properly.) *Continually* and *continuously* have similar variations in meaning. *Continually* implies a series of events with brief interruptions in between. *Continuously* implies an uninterrupted process, as in "The sun shines continuously in space and sun spots continually appear on its surface." These distinctions are not mere nitpicking. The precise use of words is essential to clarity in communication. Ambiguity and vagueness appear when words are used without attention to their precise meanings.

Some words look or sound alike but have different meanings. Others cause confusion because the distinction in meanings is not clear to all.

accept	take what is offered
except	leave out
adverse	unfavorable
averse	not inclined
advice	counsel given
advise	to give counsel

affect	to influence
effect	outcome, result
allusion	indirect reference
illusion	false impression
among	involves more than two
between	applies only to two
appraise	set a value on
apprise	inform
climactic	refers to climax
climatic	refers to climate
common	shared by two or more
mutual	interchanged, reciprocal
complement	addition to
compliment	praise
council	advisory body
counsel	give advice
differ from	variations between people or things
differ with	holding different opinions
disinterested	impartial
uninterested	having no interest in
fewer	smaller number
less	small amount
imply	indicate, suggest
infer	conclude, deduce
lay	put, place
lie	recline
many	pertains to number
much	pertains to quantity
passed	gone by
past	before
principal	primary, most important
principle	truth, law

Precision is also attained by using number, time, place, and method whenever possible.

Imprecise	Exact
Your recent letter . . .	Your letter of February 4th . . .
There are many women managers . . .	There are twenty-three women managers . . .
My flight leaves in mid morning.	My flight leaves at 10:15 A.M.
Your inquiry has been referred to the Payroll Department.	Your inquiry has been referred to Mr. Brown in the Payroll Dept.

The effective manager has respect for words used and for the audience. Words must be chosen carefully so that the meaning is clear and the audience does not have to unravel ambiguities.

Reading maketh a full man, conference a ready man, and writing an exact man.—Francis Bacon

USE FAMILIAR WORDS

As bureaucracy gave us waffling so academia gives us pedantry. The pedant never uses a familiar word if an obscure one is available. The most mundane and meretricious thought can be made to seem important if the words that express it can only be found in the footnotes to the *Oxford English Dictionary*. It was sufficient punishment for our sins to wade through the murky wording of our textbooks. Now that those days are past it should be our goal to spare each other further pain. Most ideas and proposals in business are relatively simple; abstractions do not play a large part in the daily thinking of most managers. The plain, straightforward ideas we have should be expressed in language suited to the simplicity of the thoughts.

Here are some words whose pretentiousness makes them unsuitable for most business usage. Avoid them and their kind.

Pretentious	Simple
abhor	dislike
abscond	steal

egress	exit
accelerate	increase
meretricious	valueless
mundane	common, ordinary
exigent	urgent
cognizant	aware
delineate	draw, describe
facilitate	ease, help
germane	relevant
hiatus	interruption, interval
multitudinous	many
obviate	prevent
palpable	obvious
remuneration	pay
terminate	end
utilize	use
wherewithal	means

USE STRONG VERBS

Verbs provide the dynamism that gives force and strength to our language. They offer clarity, brevity, and exactness of imagery. Changing the form of a verb weakens the sentence and obscures its meaning. Most verbs express ideas that can also be expressed by a relative noun or related adjective. Careless and/or pretentious writers weaken verbs by taking the noun or adjective that is related to a verb and combining it with another, less specific verb. For example, the verb *agree* has a noun form, *agreement*. A simple statement is, "We agreed to form a committee." A weakened form would be, "We achieved agreement relative to the forming of a committee." Notice also how weakening verbs produces obscure and verbose wording.

Strong Verb	Weakened Verb
examine	make an examination of
prepare	accomplished preparation
consider	take into consideration
study	make a study of
supervise	exercise supervision over
decide	arrive at a decision
enforce	provide enforcement
expand	achievement, enlargement, or carry out expansion

Writing simply, clearly, and forcefully is difficult, not impossible. It requires a proper respect for ideas expressed in words. It demands prior thought and organization. It means the writer must understand the audience and the purpose of the writing. Effective writing uses short sentences, simple phrasing, precise meanings, and brevity. It is a skill that must be practiced to be learned. Persons entrusted with positions in upper management must write well.

Rewrite the following memo and then turn to the next page to compare your version with a suggested revision.

From: F. R. Jones, Division Manager
To: W. R. Brown, Regional Manager

As per your request I have traveled with Bill Smith as he made his sales calls on two days of the preceding week. As you are undoubtedly aware Bill has been with our organization for approximately two years as of the present date. He has been unable to accomplish achievement of quota in any year to date. In my travels with Bill I have determined that a high proportion of his lack of successful accomplishment is due to the fact that he lacks confidence and self-esteem. Whenever he approaches a customer he does so in a manner and style that is totally antithetical to what we expect from one of our more professional salespersons. During the time that I spent with Bill I sought to make him cognizant of the deleterious and harmful effects that his behavior has upon his working relationship with our customers. In essence, his response to my observations was one of complete and total disinterest. I attempted by means of other devices to indicate my disenchantment with his performance to date but at this point in time I have been unable to detect a positive response from him. Subsequent to our discussions I have been trying to ascertain whether or not he is capable of reaching the level of accomplishment that is desired of salespersons within our oganization. It would appear that his activities and actions to date would tend to indicate that his future achievements are very problematical. In the event that you acquiesce in my conclusions please so indicate and I will endeavor to institute the proper procedures.

Rewritten memo:

From: F. R. Jones, Division Manager
  To: W. R. Brown, Regional Manager

On Monday and Tuesday of last week I traveled with Bill Smith on his sales calls. Bill has been with our company two years and has not reached his quota in either year. Part of his failure is due to a lack of confidence and self-esteem. His approach to customers is, therefore, ineffective. I pointed out this shortcoming to Bill. He was indifferent to my observation. I told him I was dissatisfied with his performance but he again responded with indifference. I do not believe Bill will ever be a successful salesman with us. If you agree, I will terminate Bill as of two weeks from Monday.

13 THE PYGMALION EFFECT

Treat people as if they are what they
ought to be, and you will help them to
become what they ought to be.
—Goethe

George Bernard Shaw was an Irishman with a taste for Greek mythology. He seized upon one of the myths of the ancient Greeks and produced a concept that is useful for parents, teachers, and managers. Shaw's play, *Pygmalion*, is based upon the story of the mythical Greek sculptor, Pygmalion, who fell in love with one of his own creations.

According to legend, Pygmalion strove to create the ideal woman in marble, as did many of the ancient Greek sculptors. The Venus de Milo and the Aphrodite of Cnidos have survived as two other examples of the effort of Greek sculptors to depict the ideal woman. Pygmalion's ideal woman in marble did not survive for an unusual reason. When the statue was finished Pygmalion had done his work so well that he fell in love with his representation of the ideal woman. His love was so intense that Pygmalion could not eat or sleep but only gaze in adoration at the marble woman whom he had created. As so often happens in Greek mythology the gods took a hand in the affairs of man. In gratitude for his creation, and out of compassion for his infatuation, the gods brought to life the statue that Pygmalion had created. The happy couple was then married, had a son, and, presumably, Pygmalion's woman was as ideal in life as she had been in stone.

In George Bernard Shaw's retelling of the myth, a Cockney flower girl is transformed into the image of a duchess. The essence of Shaw's story is that people act as they are expected to act, and become what they are expected to become. Professor Higgins transformed Eliza Doolittle by changing her external characteristics of speech and appearance. The real change occurred in the mind and personality of Eliza when she began to think and act and behave as a duchess. She became a duchess because she appeared as a duchess and people therefore treated her as a duchess. As Eliza Doolittle explains, "... the difference between a lady and flower girl is not how she behaves, but how she is treated."

Similarly, an employee can become what a manager expects that person to become. The expectations of a manager can be critical to the success or failure of subordinates. A manager's attitudes and expectations can provide either the encouragement that leads to success or the discouragement that leads to failure. The output and productivity of a group is often the mirror image of the expectations that the manager has for the group. If the manager expects and demands high performance, then it is likely to be received. If expectations and standards are set low, then the productivity of subordinates will be correspondingly low.

This principle applies on an individual as well as a group basis. In fact, in most organizations there will be few managers who extract maximum performance from all their subordinates. An evaluation of group performance usually shows a few who are exceptional, a majority that is performing near to what is expected, and a small minority who do not measure up. It was long assumed that this distribution was the result of differences in ability and/or motivation. It is only recently that we are beginning to realize that it is really due to differences in the manager's treatment of, and expectations for, subordinates. In any organization of reasonable size the new hires are quickly evaluated and the "real comers" or "fast track" people are identified fairly soon. These are the people who are seen as having those attributes that will lead to success. In most cases the high expectations for these people accurately predict what is to come. They usually are the people who rise rapidly within the organization and assume positions of responsibility before others in their age group. There is reason to believe that much of this success is due to the way they are treated rather than to their inherently superior abilities.

Numerous studies in the classroom and in business have repeatedly shown that performance is directly related to expectations. In one study teachers were told that students had been identified through testing as having superior intellectual abilities.[1] In reality they had been matched with other groups so that there was no perceivable difference in ability among the groups. At the end of the school year the children thought to be superior achieved performance levels that significantly exceeded those of the other groups. The success was due to the attitude of the teachers. The teachers perceived them as being superior and expected them to behave accordingly. The teachers treated them as superior students and the results were outstanding performances. The children responded to the expectation of the teacher so that it became a self-fulfilling prophecy.

Unquestionably such attitudes and expectations have a more powerful influence upon children than upon adults, however, this same principle has been demonstrated to apply with less, but still significant force with adults. Alfred Oberlander, in a series of experiments at the Metropolitan Life Insurance Company, demonstrated that the performance of salesmen was directly related to the expectations and demands of the managers.[2] Other studies at other companies have confirmed this conclusion.

If managers can produce exceptional performance in subordinates by their expectations and insistence on high performance, then conversely can a manager's attitude and expectations produce failure? The answer is, of course, yes. The negative feedback that a subordinate receives from a manager can produce, through loss of self-esteem and degeneration of self-confidence, the failure that the manager subconsciously expects. The subordinate then begins to act in ways that almost guarantee failure.

If this positive or negative feedback and reinforcement were deliberate tactics on the part of a manager, there would be some basis for justifying it. However, in almost all cases such behavior is entirely subconscious. The manager is not consciously treating one subordinate in a manner likely to produce success and another in a manner likely to produce failure. The critical factor is not so much what is said but how it is said; not so much what is done, but how it is done. The manager's body language, facial expression, tone of voice, and other nonverbal signals tell the subordinate how he/she is regarded by the manager and what level of success or failure the manager truly expects. There also seems to be a tendency among managers to more clearly transmit negative feelings than positive. Perhaps this is because, as with other emotions, negative attitudes are more powerful and visible than those that are positive.

It is important to remember that the critical element is the true underlying attitude of the manager. There are managers who talk in terms of success and high performance but whose achievements do not correspond to their talk. They are much like the athlete who "talks a good game." In the locker room such an athlete sounds and acts like a world champion. On the playing field where inadequacy cannot be disguised his performance fails to match his locker room talk. A manager who lacks self-confidence and the inner strength that comes from knowing that the job will get done will transmit these negative impulses to subordinates regardless of what is said. The level of success will be consistent with a basic attitude and not with words.

Managers can also undermine performance by establishing standards that are unrealistically high. When standards are set so high that they are impossible to achieve, rather than striving and coming close, most people will cease to try and their performances will fall substantially below what they are capable of. The expectation that a manager has for the group should be consistent with the ability of the group. However, in order for maximum performance to be achieved there should always be some "stretch" in the setting of objectives. The attitude of the manager should be one of confident expectation that with a concerted effort high goals can be achieved.

The most interesting aspect of the Pygmalion effect is that the high expectations that an effective manager has for a group are usually based not upon superior qualities in the group but rather in self-confidence. The manager feels competent and capable of leading the group to outstanding achievement. It is very likely that this attitude becomes the catalyst for the success of the group, which will recognize the confidence of the manager, acknowledge his/her competence, and perform in the manner expected.

If a group is to function effectively and achieve high standards of performance, it is essential that the manager actively develop the ability of subordinates. The subordinates must be given an opportunity to learn and grow within their job experience. The manager must function as a teacher, mentor, and role model. The manager must carefully recognize the abilities and shortcomings of associates and work with them to enhance their strengths and overcome their weaknesses. The role of teacher is always a part of an effective manager's plan. It is this type of personal involvement that makes possible the self-fulfilling prophecy, which is the essential element in the Pygmalion effect. The self-fulfilling prophecy does not occur because the manager expects it to happen or wants it to happen. It occurs because the manager expects something to happen and then works with the individual or group to make sure that it does happen. Professor Higgins did not turn Eliza Doolittle into a lady by wanting her to become one. He spent days, weeks, and months working with her to alter her speech, her dress, her appearance, and her behavior. The end result was that she was treated as a lady and became a lady. If Professor Higgins had merely wanted or expected this outcome it would not have occurred. A manager who wants and expects high performance must work with each subordinate to ensure that such performance is achieved.

The manager who demands high performance will receive it only if the demand is accompanied by a personal involvement with each subordinate in the development of the subordinate's talent. The effective manager will identify areas of weakness that each subordinate has and work to overcome those weaknesses. The manager will identify strengths and will build upon those strengths to make an even stronger individual. The effective manager will clearly communicate the goals and expectations for each person and develop an action plan so that success can be mapped out ahead of time. It is this combination of expectation and involvement that creates the self-fulfilling prophecy.

One of your major responsibilities as a manager is to have a positive attitude toward each of your subordinates and to develop the abilities of those subordinates consistent with that positive attitude. The effective manager is never satisfied if even one member of the group is performing below par. Each subordinate should represent a challenge to the manager to produce outstanding performance. The effective manager settles for nothing less.

EXERCISES

These exercises are in two parts. Do not do Part II until Part I has been completed.

Part I

List your subordinates and indicate on the scale provided their customary levels of performance.

			Performance Scale		
Subordinate	Poor	Fair	Average	Superior	Outstanding
	1	2	3	4	5

1.

2.

Subordinate	Poor 1	Fair 2	Average 3	Superior 4	Outstanding 5
3.					
4.					
5.					
6.					
7.					
8.					

Part II

List your subordinates and analyze your attitude toward each of them. In each case try to recall specific behavior of yours that revealed that attitude.

Subordinates	Basic Attitude
1.	
2.	
3.	
4.	
5.	
6.	
7.	
8.	

NOTES

1. Robert Rosenthal and Lenore Jacobson, *Pygmalion in the Classroom* (New York: Holt, Rinehart and Winston, 1968), pp. 61-71.

2. "Jamesville Branch Office (A)," MET003A, and "Jamesville Branch Office (B)," MET003B, Sterling Institute, 1969.

14 PERFORMANCE APPRAISAL

L et's get it out in the open. Everyone hates performance appraisals. Everyone is uncomfortable in an appraisal session. This is
true of both managers and subordinates. No one likes to judge or be
judged. The consequence is that performance appraisals are conducted with little preparation, too quickly, and with little positive
effect.

The problem could be partly solved if managers understood
that the purpose of a performance appraisal is not to judge the work
of the subordinate. Whatever judgments are required should have
been made while the work was being done. An employee should not
have to wait for an annual appraisal session to discover what the
manager thinks of the work that was done.

The only real purpose of an appraisal session is to *improve
performance*! That is why the manager and subordinate sit down
together. They should be engaged in a mutual analysis of where the
employee stands at that moment and how performance can be
improved, to the benefit of both the employee and the company. The
focus should be on the future, not the past.

A properly conducted performance appraisal provides a subordinate with an accurate and objective view of how his/her work
is viewed by the manager. From such an interview the subordinate

should learn precisely what is expected, and action plans should be developed to achieve those goals. The subordinate should also receive an assessment of strengths and weaknesses and a determination of the training needed to further develop his/her abilities. The subordinate should receive some guidance in personal development and the achievement of career goals, as well as a motivational stimulus that provides the psychic energy needed to improve performance.

The reverse side of that coin is that an improperly conducted performance appraisal can be extremely destructive to the morale and performance of the subordinate. Instead of creating a positive climate for improved performance it can poison the atmosphere and critically impair the ability of the manager and subordinate to work together. In extreme cases, a poorly conducted performance appraisal can lead a subordinate to seek other employment and cost the company and the manager the services of a productive employee. In order to avoid these dangers many managers are willing to forego the opportunity for positive results and conduct totally innocuous interviews. Either consciously or subconsciously they are so apprehensive of doing the wrong thing that they elect to do nothing. Such an interview seldom rises above the level of, "You're doing a fine job and I know that next year we can expect the same thing from you." Such interviews are helpful to neither the employee nor the supervisor and are frequently counterproductive because they cause the subordinate to lose respect for the manager.

The effective manager will recognize the possible dangers that lie within a performance appraisal but will not be deterred from seizing the opportunity. There is an obligation to function as a manager and to conduct performance appraisals so that employees, the company, and the manager derive benefits from them. The manager will also recognize that in an appraisal interview the subordinate may be uncomfortable. The manager should recognize the emotional state of the subordinate and adjust to it, with an attitude of calm, nonaccusatory evaluation. If at all possible, the approach should be one of a mutual investigation of the situation, a determination of the essential factors, and agreement upon the evaluation of those factors.

The manager may also be uncomfortable during the performance appraisal. Few of us are so secure in our self-image or so completely egocentric that we can comfortably pass judgement on other people without feeling twinges of conscience. Most of us are still responsive to the Biblical injunction, "Judge not, lest ye also be judged." Too many managers react to their discomfort by being either abrupt and dictatorial or soft and squishy. In either case the manager attempts to end the interview as quickly as possible and thereby end the discomfort. The effective manager, however, will not allow the discomfort to affect the interview. In much the same way as an actor overcomes stage fright so a manager will overcome the feeling of discomfort that exists during the performance appraisal.

Some years ago the General Electric Company did an intensive study[1] of their performance appraisal program and came to the following conclusions:

—Criticism has a negative effect on achievement of goals.

—Praise has little effect one way or the other.

—Performance improves most when specific goals are established.

—Defensiveness resulting from critical appraisal produces inferior performance.

—Coaching should be a day-to-day, not a once-a-year, activity.

—Mutual goal setting, not criticism, improves performance.

—Interviews designed primarily to improve a man's performance should not at the same time weigh his salary or promotion in the balance.

—Participation by the employee in the goal-setting procedure helps produce favorable results.

A properly conducted performance appraisal will require preparation on the part of both the manager and the subordinate. Both parties should review the objectives that were set for the subordinate at the beginning of the year. This should be done separately, with successes and failures noted. Each should then develop an overall evaluation of the year's performance. The manager should have a clear picture of the various tasks or projects to which the subordinate was assigned and the manner in which they were accomplished. The manager should carefully review the efforts of the subordinate during the year and list strengths and weaknesses.

An effective technique for opening the appraisal session is to ask for the subordinate's own evaluation of the year's performance. If the year's objectives were properly written, the subordinate's appraisal of performance should correspond closely to the manager's. When a difference of opinion occurs it will almost always be due to an objective that was vaguely written. Either the task itself was not clearly described or, as is more common, not properly quantified. If there is a difference of opinion, the manager should listen to the subordinate's position and withhold judgment until further into the interview.

Any system for performance appraisal carries with it certain advantages and disadvantages. The advantage in setting objectives is that the performance appraisal is based upon specific objectives that can be measured, without having recourse to subjective opinion. If the objectives are prepared properly, at the end of the year there should be no question as to whether or not they have been achieved. When a performance appraisal is based upon specific objectives the subjective opinion of the manager should not enter into the discussion. An objective appraisal interview avoids the arguments that are prompted by statements such as:

"Your work is acceptable but your attitude needs improvement."

"I have no complaints about your work but you should learn to get along better with the other people in the department."

"Your work is satisfactory but you really don't seem to take much of an interest in the company."

"Why can't you be more of a team player; where is your team spirit?"

Managers all too often make these kinds of subjective statements in performance appraisals. Evaluating objectives and their accomplishment lessens subjectivity in performance appraisals and presumably eliminates statements of attitude.

The disadvantage of using a system of objectives to evaluate performance is that there is no way to objectively analyze the quality of work. There is no provision for the person who accomplishes assigned tasks in the time allotted, but does so in a last minute burst of activity that disrupts and interferes with the activities of other people in the department. The effective manager therefore must find a way to evaluate those aspects of an employee's performance that are not adequately described in the listed objectives. The manager can do this by focusing on procedures that will tend to enlist the subordinate's agreement and to lessen the possibility for arguments.

First, the manager's comments should be descriptive, not accusatory. The focus should be on helping the employee see himself as others do. An appropriate comment might be, "What do you suppose is the effect on the other people in the department when one week before an assignment is due you are working at such a furious and frantic pace?" The intent should be to help the subordinate see himself in an objective and unemotional way and to reflect upon the effect of his actions. The manager should serve as a mirror, forcing the subordinate to see how disruptive behavior affects the other people in the department.

Second, the manager should focus on what the subordinate does and what the effects are, rather than on emotional or mental states the subordinate might have. There is little to be accomplished by trying to analyze the reasons for particular behavior patterns. The manager should not fall into the trap of attempting to become the employee's analyst. It serves little purpose for the manager to talk about poor attitude, lack of motivation, or insecurity. The natural reaction by a subordinate, who hears these or similar phrases from a manager, is to become defensive. Most subordinates resent attempts by their managers to describe emotional states. In this instance, fairness is on the side of the subordinate. It is not possible for a manager to accurately assess the emotional causes of employee behavior. The manager is on far safer and more productive ground by focusing on visible behavior rather than on some unseen mental condition.

The manager who feels that the employee does not have the proper attitude, should ask, "How is this condition manifested?" What behavior is specific evidence of poor attitude? Is the employee habitually tardy in arriving for work; is work continually turned in that needs to be corrected and redone? Does the employee insist on doing only his own work with never a thought of assisting others? Specific behavior can be pointed out to the employee and an explanation of that behavior solicited.

Finally, the manager should be specific and not general in comments. It is not enough to say, "That proposal you wrote was poorly done." In order for this type of feedback to be effective it must be specific; it must show exactly *how* it was poorly done. Was the research behind the proposal inadequate? Was the language in the proposal confusing or misleading? Did part of the proposal wander into areas that were not directly relevant to the main issue? Was the description of the problem inadequate or ambiguous? Were the conclusions incomplete or impractical? This is the type of specific evaluation that is useful to the employee. Remember, as a manager you are attempting to change behavior, which does not occur when a person is defensive, resentful, or argumentative. It can only take place when a person acknowledges the validity of the problem and is motivated to do something about it. The beginning of this process of behavioral change is the identification of specific behavior that is nonproductive and an awareness of the effect of that behavior upon other people.

The manager should, wherever possible, place things in a positive light. The emphasis should be on what the employee can do differently to produce more effective behavior, rather than on what has been done badly. Comments such as, "You never should have done that," or, "It was a mistake for you to...," generate resentment rather than cooperation. It's usually better to phrase comments in a positive way. For example, "It probably would have been better if you...," "A more effective way might have been to...." This approach will tend to reduce the resentment in what is seen to be a judgmental situation and to produce a higher level of cooperation.

Every employee has a right to at least one formal appraisal session each year. This is a commitment that a company specifically makes to its employees, and it is each manager's responsibility to fulfill that commitment by conducting well-prepared appraisal sessions that are productive, objective, and positive.

In summary:

- Don't criticize
- Don't praise
- Set specific, measurable goals
- Provide daily coaching
- Don't combine salary review and performance appraisal
- Focus on behavior and its effects, not on emotional or mental states
- Be specific in your comments
- Use positive phrases
- Prepare properly
- Adjust to the emotional climate of the session

The following list of questions may be helpful as an aid to developing your skill in conducting effective performance appraisals. After each interview ask yourself these questions and analyze your answers to see where improvement can be made.

- Was your appraisal based on objective data?
- Did the employee agree with the appraisal?
- If not, why not?
- Were shortcomings identified?
- Was an action plan devised to correct shortcomings?
- What sort of atmosphere was created?
- What did you do well?
- What did you do poorly?
- How can you do better next time?

NOTE

1. Herbert H. Meyer, Emmanuel Kay, and John R. P. French, Jr., "Split Roles in Performance Appraisal," *Harvard Business Review* (January-February 1965).

15 TRAINING AND DEVELOPMENT

G ood managers are good teachers. Think of the best manager you ever had. If ten different people were asked to do so, they would probably describe ten managers considerably different in appearance, management style, leadership ability, motivational techniques, and other characteristics of a competent manager. However, a statement that would probably be made about each one is "I really learned from that person." This distinguishes the boss that we remember from those whom we would just as soon forget. As in school, the teacher that we remember is the one that was tough but fair and demanded the best from us.

Many times the most well-remembered managers are not the most congenial people. They may not be polished, suave, or sophisticated but they are effective teachers. This is the one distinguishing characteristic of all good managers. The good manager is a good teacher. As a manager you now have responsibility for teaching the people who report to you. You must teach them in two different areas. First, you must teach them the skills of their present job, and how to improve on them. Second, you must teach them what must be learned for their next step up the promotion ladder. You are therefore responsible for both the training and the developing of your people. How you go about this task and how well it is accomplished will to a large measure determine your success or failure as a manager.

Many companies, especially those committed to a program of promotion from within, measure a manager's effectiveness by how well subordinates are trained and developed. In such companies a manager is seldom considered for promotion unless he/she demonstrably improves the working effectiveness of subordinates and has fully prepared at least one as a successor. This emphasis upon training and development achieves a number of objectives. First, it ensures that employee productivity will be kept high; each employee receives the training that is needed to function effectively. Second, promotions, transfers, terminations, and retirements will cause little or no dislocation in the managerial ranks; there will always be an adequate replacement for each manager who leaves. Third, employee morale will be high as opportunities for learning and advancement will constantly occur.

The effective manager, therefore, understands and accepts responsibility as a teacher. However, to enunciate general principles is one thing, but to put them into practice is another. Once this responsibility has been accepted how does the manager actually go about determining the training and development needs of subordinates, and how to fill those needs? Let us consider the area of training first and later that of development. Note the difference between training and developing. Training focuses on specific skills that an employee needs in order to function effectively in the present job. Development focuses not upon skills but upon the knowledge and techniques that are required at the next higher level of responsibility.

TRAINING

In order to train your workers, it is first necessary to be very clear about exactly what you expect of them. The questions that must be resolved before training can begin are:

- What exactly are my people expected to do?
- How are they expected to do it?
- What equipment is needed?
- What skills are required?

- At what level of proficiency?
- What is each person's present skill level?

Once you have listed all the tasks that your employees are expected to perform you should rank them in descending order of importance. When you have a firm grasp on exactly what is expected of your people, you can evaluate them and determine the performance gap for each of them. In other words, you measure the gap between actual performance and what you expect. The outcome should result in a diagnosis for each of your subordinates that indicates strengths and weaknesses, and tells you which gaps in skills, techniques, or knowledge require your attention first. You should prepare a program for each employee that describes first, the skill or technique that needs to be developed; second, the procedure by which the training will occur; and third, the time span for the training. This must be done for each subordinate since each one has a different level of ability and capacity for learning.

Once a training program has been decided upon, the manager should meet with the employees individually to review the programs. They should understand that the programs are tailored to their particular situations and are designed to help them function more effectively in their present jobs. It is during this interview that the manager should help each employee understand how his/her job fits into the total responsibility for the department. This is especially important, of course, for younger employees, but is equally so for older employees. It is disheartening to note how often a senior employee will not know how his/her job fits in with the mission of the department. It is necessary to provide this frame of reference so that the employee understands and fits the parts together to form a unified whole, instead of learning isolated bits and pieces of actions and behavior. An effective manager will not neglect this essential introduction to the training process. The process by which a person learns is fairly well established, whether it is training for a specific job, an academic subject, or a sport such as tennis. There are five steps in the learning process:

1. Motivation
2. Instruction
3. Practice
4. Reinforcement
5. Feedback

Motivation

Someone who does not care to learn will not learn. In fact, as teachers have known for many years, one cannot really teach another anything. All that a teacher can do is *help* someone to learn. Unless the student or trainee is motivated to learn, any effort expended on instruction will be wasted. And, of course, the higher the motivation the faster and more effective the learning will be. Before beginning any training program make sure that sufficient motivation exists so that real learning can take place. If the trainee's attitude is one of resistance or apathy then the manager must either motivate that individual to want to learn, or accept his/her present level of skill and learn to live with it. If the skill level is not acceptable then termination or transfer is recommended.

Instruction

Assuming proper motivation, the initial instruction should be as simple and basic as possible, providing information that allows the trainee to take one step forward at a time. One should be careful not to overload the trainee with too many bits of information, or specific tasks, and expect him/her to accomplish or understand all of them in a short time. The most effective instruction concentrates on the most important skill or understanding that is to be learned, breaks it down into smaller parts, and presents the information to the trainee in a sequential manner. The rate of instruction should be based upon the speed at which the employee learns. Remember, you are trying to change human behavior; this cannot be done all at once. Change one thing at a time before moving on to the next.

Practice

The employee should be given an opportunity to practice what has been learned. The practice at first should be in a non-critical setting. If the manager is teaching sales skills, then the practice or application of those skills should occur first in a role-playing situation that does not involve the stress of dealing with a customer. Before practice sessions the manager should make sure that the trainee has received instruction sufficient to allow him/her to function reasonably well within that first practice session. Do not rush this process. Placing a trainee in a practice session without adequate preparation virtually ensures failure. Initial failure of this kind can cause frustration and substantially reduce the motivational level.

One must learn, by doing the thing, for though you think
you know it you have no certainty, until you try.
—Sophocles

Reinforcement

The employee should receive reinforcement in the form of encouragement or praise. This should not be overdone, but as the employee shows progress it should be noted and commented on favorably by the manager.

Feedback

In order for the total process to be effective there must be feedback to the employee. This feedback should consist of specific comments that show how close the employee is coming to the expected standard of performance. It is difficult for a person to improve without knowing how much improvement is expected. Once the trainee has gained sufficient confidence through positive reinforcement the manager should not hesitate to tell the subordinate when progress is being made and when it is not.

The five step process of learning continues for each task, skill, or understanding that is expected of a trainee. When one skill or one level of proficiency has been mastered, the trainee is moved to another skill or the next level. Assuming that the motivation continues, the manager goes back to the instructional stage of the process and begins over again with each new step.

It is helpful for both the manager and the trainee to understand that learning does not take place at a constant rate. Whether one is involved in a motor skill or an abstract understanding, learning usually occurs in a series of jumps. A leap to a plateau is followed by a period of little apparent growth and then a jump to the next plateau. It is necessary that both the manager and the subordinate understand this process so that when the trainee is showing little progress it is understood that he/she is merely at a plateau and preparing for the next jump. If this process is not understood both the manager and the trainee are likely to become discouraged and the effectiveness of the training will be lessened.

DEVELOPMENT

Once the initial training programs have been implemented the manager should focus on the development of those subordinates whose levels of skills and abilities indicate their potential for promotion. The effective manager will employ any or all of the following five different techniques for developing skills of promotable subordinates.

Delegation

First, the manager can begin to delegate responsibility to promotable subordinates. Exercising responsibility will allow a subordinate to grow both in understanding the job and in the ability to deal with other people. The manager must keep in mind the principle that one delegates but does not abdicate. The performance of subordinates must be monitored. Occasionally a subordinate must be allowed to make mistakes and correct them alone without intervention from the manager. This, however, can only be done when the consequences of those mistakes will not be too severe.

Coaching

Second, a manager can use the technique of coaching to provide guidance to subordinates. Rather than directly delegating responsibility, the manager assigns part of a task to a subordinate and then personally assists him in the accomplishment of that task. This process allows the subordinate to make mistakes and have them corrected before serious consequences occur. The manager must walk a delicate line between giving too much assistance and giving too little.

Special Assignment

Third, a manager can make special assignments to selected subordinates. A special assignment will usually develop out of an unusual situation or a new problem facing the department. The assignment might involve the development of a plan to reduce costs or improve efficiency, or a training program for new hires, or similar responsibilities. A special assignment is usually a one-time responsibility and can be effectively used to develop the skills and experience of a subordinate.

Job Rotation

Fourth, the manager can use job rotation to give subordinates experience in areas outside their primary responsibility. A job rotation can be a permanent assignment (lateral transfer), or it may be a temporary assignment. The purpose is to expose the employee to different problems and situations and provide him/her with a wider understanding of company operations. Many times job rotation involves the cooperation of another supervisor, and is frequently done on a quid pro quo basis.

Understudy

Fifth, a manager can appoint an assistant. The understudy chosen is acknowledged as the person who will logically succeed the manager. Everyone knows that this succession is taking place and that the understudy is being prepared for the position. This should only be done when the understudy is head and shoulders above the other subordinates. In taking this route the manager must be careful of its effect upon the motivation of the other subordinates.

EXERCISES

List each of your subordinates and indicate specific needs for training and development.

Subordinate	Training Needs	Development Needs	Program
1.			
2.			
3.			

Subordinate	Training Needs	Development Needs	Program
4.			
5.			
6.			
7.			
8.			

16 HIRING

A newly appointed manager faces two separate learning situations—learning about the job and learning about subordinates. A new manager must quickly assess the strengths and weaknesses of the subordinates, knowing that one must work with what has been inherited.

In most instances it is only after the manager has been in place for a while that the necessity for recruiting and hiring appears. It is at this point that the manager can begin to put an individual stamp on the personnel of the group. As a new manager, you have the opportunity and the challenge of selecting people considered to fit best into the organization and you should understand that the persons selected will be looked at carefully by your own superiors. Shortcomings of inherited subordinates can be blamed on previous managers. Shortcomings in the people you hire will be your responsibility. The selection of capable people is one of the distinguishing characteristics of a successful manager. The quality of people that you hire will have a significant impact upon your own success in the present job and on opportunities for further advancement.

To hire properly, a manager must devote sufficient time and attention to the task. It is not a job that can be done quickly or in odd moments snatched from other responsibilities. The wise manager, knowing that a mistake in hiring will cause problems well into the future, will have a carefully thought out program with which to hire competent people.

A program for hiring the right people breaks down into two phases: recruiting and interviewing. If you are a field sales manager or in some other position outside the home office, it will probably be your responsibility to do both the recruiting and the hiring of new personnel. If your job is within the home office, the recruiting aspect will probably be the responsibility of the personnel department. In either situation it is essential that the manager do careful planning before the recruiting process begins. The planning should involve a thorough analysis of the available position and a specific description of the type of person best able to fill it.

The manager should first analyze the job to be filled by listing its specific tasks and responsibilities, considering carefully whether the job requires primary involvement with people, with ideas, or with things. The manager should analyze how much interaction is required with other people in the department, who those people are, and what sort of personalities they represent. Does the work involve contact with customers or suppliers, and if so, is it face-to-face or over the telephone? Questions that the managers should be asking and answering at this stage are:

- What are the specific responsibilities of the job?
- What experience is necessary to fulfill those responsibilities?
- What abilities or talents are required?
- What skills must the applicant already have and what skills can be taught?
- Is the position a dead-end job or is it a training slot for future advancement?
- What are the appealing aspects of the job and what are the discouraging aspects?
- Is it a routine position or does it require imagination and innovation?

Once the job has been thoroughly analyzed the manager can begin to draw a profile of the person best suited for that job. The manager should list the qualifications and attributes that are necessary to successfully fill the position. As many qualities as possible should be listed. Once a complete profile has been obtained the manager should place these qualities in order of priority. When the interviewing stage is reached, the manager will find that no one matches the profile exactly. The people that should receive serious consideration are those who most closely meet the high priority requirements.

If the manager is in the field and responsible for his/her own recruiting, the key requirements for the job should be summarized and included in an advertisement to be placed in the local newspapers. The opening should also be publicized through current employees, personal contacts, and other sources where suitable candidates may be found.

The manager working in a home office through the personnel department should provide a description of the job and of the ideal candidate. The manager should also meet with the personnel recruiter to thoroughly discuss the position and the type of person that is being sought. It is essential that the personnel recruiter have a clear picture of exactly the kind of person that the manager is seeking. The more specific and detailed the information that the recruiter has, the closer the actual candidates will come to the profile that the manager has constructed.

The process of communication with the personnel department should continue until an applicant has been selected and hired. After each applicant has been interviewed the manager should discuss that person with the recruiter, indicating where the applicant matched the profile and where there were deviations. This type of feedback provides the recruiter with a better focus on the type of applicant that should be sought.

THE INTERVIEW ITSELF

The field manager should never interview applicants at home or in the applicant's home. If a regional office is not available, then the interviews should be conducted in a motel meeting room. The manager should reserve the room for a specific day and schedule the applicants during that day, with a minimum of one hour allocated to each first interview.

Whether conducted in the field or in the office the interviews should be essentially the same. The manager should have three primary goals for the interview:

1. Obtaining as much pertinent information as possible about the applicant.

2. Providing essential information about the company and the job that is to be filled.
3. Creating a favorable impression of both oneself and the company so that if a job offer is made it will be accepted eagerly.

The first few minutes of the interview should be devoted to placing the applicant at ease, but this period should not be unnecessarily prolonged. In this situation, managers should remember that they are creating, consciously or not, an image of themselves and of the company. That image must be one of competence, professionalism, and quiet enthusiasm.

The manager should have a copy of the applicant's resume and/or employment application. The information provided should avoid the necessity for many closed-end questions commonly asked in interviews, such as, "Where was your last job?," "How long did you work there?," and "What was your title?" Except where specific pieces of information are missing the manager should focus on open-ended questions that do not allow the applicant to give short, factual answers. These kinds of questions force the applicant to reveal the extent of knowledge, amount of experience, attitudes, biases, personality, and other information that provide a picture of his/her suitability as an employee.

Among the open-ended questions that the manager might ask are:

- Describe one thing in your last job that was done particularly well.

- What major problems did you encounter in your last job?

- How did you overcome those problems?

- What kind of work do you find most enjoyable?

- What kind of work do you least enjoy?

- What kind of people do you enjoy working with?

- What attributes do you look for in a supervisor?

- What are the aspects of a job that are most important to you?

- What are your objectives and responsibilities in your present job?

- How do you spend your time in your present job?

- Why are you looking for a different job?

- Describe your career plan.

- If you were independently wealthy and didn't have to work, what would you do?

During this period of interrogation the manager should avoid leading questions that begin with such statements as "Do you agree that . . . ," or "Are you in favor of . . . ?" Such questions indicate to the applicant the type of answers that the manager is looking for and the shrewd applicant will tailor his/her answers according to what he/she senses the manager wants.

In asking the open-ended questions listed above the manager should give the applicant sufficient time to answer in detail. Do not cut short the replies of the applicant; usually, the longer a person talks the more that is revealed. Longer answers also give the manager an opportunity to evaluate the mental processes of the applicant by noting whether the replies are organized, sequential, and concise while still being complete, or if they are vague, rambling, and imprecise.

The astute manager will not be made uncomfortable during periods of silence. In fact, this time should be used to draw from the applicant remarks that might not otherwise be made. When an applicant appears to have completed an answer, but it seems that not all has been revealed, the manager should allow a period of silence. If he gives the impression that he is waiting for the applicant to continue, then the pressure will build. If the manager is patient, the applicant will resume talking and in many cases reveal attitudes, information, or beliefs that were being concealed.

When the manager has obtained sufficient information from the applicant, the process should be reversed and the applicant provided with information. The manager should describe in detail the position that is to be filled, what is expected of the person who will fill that position, the basic details about the company itself, and whatever compensation and benefit information is suitable at that time. The manager should present this information in a positive, straightforward manner so that the applicant has a clear and favorable image of the job and the company. When discussing compensation and benefits the specific data should be presented in a forthright manner. Regardless of the manager's personal feelings about the adequacy or inadequacy of compensation or benefits, there should be no hint of hesitancy or apology in stating what the wages and the benefits are. The information about compensation should be presented as an accomplished fact with confidence that it will be regarded as more than adequate. The manager must give no hint that anything the company offers is less than outstanding.

The applicant should be given every opportunity to ask questions about the job, the responsibilities, or the company. The manager should answer these questions fully and in detail without disclosing confidential company data. This period of questioning by the applicant also gives the manager further insight into the attitudes and beliefs of the applicant. At the end of the interview the manager should clearly indicate that the applicant will be contacted within a specific period of time to learn whether or not he/she is still under consideration for the position and if so, where and with whom further interviews will be conducted.

As soon as the applicant leaves, the manager should jot down a summary of the interview. The notes should indicate the particular strengths and weaknesses of the applicant and areas that need further investigation should the applicant be called in for additional interviews. In considering those applicants with whom further interviews should be conducted, the manager should understand that much of the decision making involved is going to depend upon intuition. The process of selection really involves a process of elimination. Those applicants who are obviously unsuitable are immediately rejected. The few outstanding applicants should be set aside for future interviews. The bulk of applicants in the middle, or gray area, should then be reviewed carefully, eliminating those whose weaknesses outweigh their strengths. The end result should be a rather small group of applicants who appear to have the qualities necessary for success in the job. Each of their resumes and applications should be reviewed in detail and specific plans and questions prepared for the second round of interviews. Depending upon the job and the department the interviewing should continue until the final selection is made and an applicant hired.

In coming to a final decision and selecting one applicant for a job offer, most experienced managers have learned not to disregard their intuition. It is very seldom that one applicant is so superior to the others that the decision makes itself. Most often a manager will be faced with two or three applicants, all with varying strengths or weaknesses, and none of whom is perfect. The final decision becomes one of weighing all the factors and subjectively selecting one applicant. At this stage intuition is very important. Do not hire someone who is producing a negative reaction in your viscera. If you go against your instinct, almost invariably that person will prove to be a problem. That is not to say that every person to whom you react favorably will prove to be outstanding. Positive reactions will produce many disappointments but negative reactions will prove to be almost 100 percent accurate.

CONDUCTING A LAWFUL EMPLOYMENT INTERVIEW

A manager has a responsibility to conduct an interview in a manner consistent with the laws regarding equal opportunity and discrimination. These are a series of laws stemming from the Civil Rights Act of 1964, and including the Equal Pay Act of 1963, the Age Discrimination in Employment Act, and Executive Order 11246. Without getting into the specifics of each one of these acts, and others passed by state legislatures, the intent of this legislation is to prevent companies from discriminating in their hiring practices because of age, sex, race, religion, national origin, or physical handicap. The manager conducting an employment interview should be aware of restrictions upon the types of questions asked or information sought. Court rulings regarding discrimination in employment have placed numerous constraints upon an employer in seeking information about job applicants.

It is obvious that an employer may not ask an applicant about his/her race, age, or religion, but less obvious are the restraints upon other questions that would indirectly provide information in these areas. The courts have also ruled that the qualifications that employers set for their applicants must be directly related to the particular jobs involved and can in no way be used to select out applicants on a discriminatory basis. It is in attempting to adhere to these guidelines that some managers encounter difficulty. Questions that a manager may consider to be quite innocent and nondiscriminatory may be viewed otherwise by an applicant or a judge, should a discrimination suit be filed.

In order to protect oneself and one's company the manager should consider the questions being asked and the information being sought to determine if there is a potential conflict with the equal opportunity laws. If qualifications are established for a particular job, then the manager must be certain that those qualifications have relevance to that job. In other words, if a college degree is required, then the manager must be able to show that that requirement is *essential* to the person holding the job. If such a requirement is not directly related to the job, then someone might infer that it is an attempt to screen out minority applicants who have less opportunity to attend college. Sex may be a legitimate qualification for hiring an attendant for a men's room or a ladies' room, but aside from these two extreme examples, there are few situations in which sex would be a legitimate qualification. The intent of the various laws and court decisions is to prohibit the denial of employment to people because of their age, their sex, or their race. The manager should avoid asking questions or seeking information that might allow someone to infer that discrimination is occurring. Areas to avoid include the following:

—*Arrest and conviction records*—viewed as discriminatory because blacks and other minorities have a higher percentage of arrests than nonminorities.

—*Garnishment records*—considered discriminatory for the same reason.

—*Credit references.*

—*Marital status*—unless it is asked of both men and women.

—*Child care problems*—unless the question is asked of both men and women.

—*Contraceptive practices*—questions such as, "What kind of birth control methods do you use?"

—*Plans to have children.*

—*Unwed motherhood.*

—*Age.*

—*Height and weight.*

—*Education*—unless it can be shown to be directly related to the job.

—*Fluency in English*—unless it is an important job requirement.

—*Availability for weekend work*—employers are required to make reasonable allowances for employees whose religion requires observances or practices that may differ from the employer's standards, schedules, or other employment conditions.

—*Experience*—only valid when it is essential to the function of the job.

—*Skill requirements*—cannot be justified when the job can be quickly learned.

—*Military discharge*—questions about military experience or training are permissible but not questions about the type of discharge received. Such questions about the type of discharge are considered discriminatory because a higher proportion of other than honorable discharges are given to minorities.

—*Citizenship*—may be established, and if the applicant is not a citizen it is also proper to ask whether he/she has a working visa. There should be no questions about the country of origin.

This listing of possible problem areas is by no means complete. If as a manager you have a specific question relating to possible antidiscrimination laws, you should contact the company personnel department for an answer.

In general the wise manager will avoid questions or statements that might be construed as discriminatory. All information sought from an applicant should relate directly to the job involved and should apply equally to all applicants regardless of race, religion, sex, or age. The prudent manager will maintain a consistent approach throughout the interviewing process and avoid possible problems.

EXERCISES

To prepare yourself for a hiring interview list five open-ended questions that you would ask of any applicant. These questions should be different from those listed in this chapter.

1.

2.

3.

4.

5.

17 FIRING

The most difficult and distressing task a manager has is to fire a subordinate. Regardless of the justification no manager is comfortable in this situation. To deprive a person of a means of earning a living is a serious matter, and some managers are so intimidated by the consequences of termination that they do everything in their power to avoid having to make such a decision. They will retain unproductive or disruptive employees rather than fire them. Some managers will even seek to promote someone who should be fired, as a way of ridding themselves of a troublesome employee. The results of such behavior are harmful to the manager, the company, and most of all, the employee.

Every manager has a responsibility to ensure that each subordinate is a useful, productive worker. Those employees who are not performing adequately should be given every opportunity through training and practice to improve their performance. Those whose lack of innate ability makes it impossible for them to match performance standards should be offered less demanding work. Those who fail to measure up because of lack of interest or effort should be terminated.

It is obviously unfair to the company to retain an unproductive worker. It is just as unfair to the employee. Almost every unmotivated, uninterested employee would be better off in another job in another company where personal interests and aspirations might better be served. Many times it is only inertia that keeps an employee in a job for which he/she is not suited.

The interests of both the employee and the company are best served by a termination that forces the employee to seek more compatible employment. No one enjoys going to work every day knowing that his/her work is not being done properly. The long-term psychological effects of this kind of situation are very harmful. It is unfair for a company to retain an employee in a job where he/she is unproductive and thereby, unhappy. The only satisfactory solution is for the manager to accept responsibility and fire the employee, allowing a fresh start with another company.

A number of years ago I was a newly appointed sales manager for a division of a large corporation. In reviewing the sales records, I noticed that Nick, a salesman in Florida, had been with the company for two years and had a decline in sales for each of those years. His region was without a manager at the time and I decided to go to Flordia and travel with him. My preliminary decision was to terminate him unless I discovered some unusual extenuating circumstances. As I was arranging my schedule, I received a report that Nick had been a day late in setting up a booth at an exhibit for which he was responsible. In addition he was rarely at the booth during the remaining two days of the exhibit but had been very active in hammering on the hotel room doors of two women sales reps at three A.M. I decided that the trip to Flordia was not needed and that I would fire Nick forthwith.

Although I had been a first-line field sales manager and had hired many people I had never actually fired anyone. I was kind of looking forward to it. I prepared in my mind a devastating indictment of Nick's sales record and behavior at the exhibit. My verdict was to be guilty on all counts and the judgment was to be execution by firing squad. I had my secretary call Nick and tell him to be in my office the next morning.

At 10:30 the following morning, my secretary called on the intercom and said that Nick was in the reception area. I told her to send him in and quickly ran through my denunciation as I turned to get my first look at Nick. The door opened and Nick entered, turning slightly sideways to get through the door. Nick was about the same height and width as a jukebox. I found out later that, although somewhat less than medium height, Nick weighed 245 pounds and had been a heavyweight wrestler and weight lifter in college. Nick settled into the chair on the other side of my desk, threatening to split the shoulder seams on his jacket as he did so. Grasping the situation with rapier-like speed, I changed tactics. Forgetting the fierce outrage I had been ready to unleash, I began to talk to Nick in a calm, older brother manner. I reasoned that if matters stayed dispassionate Nick would be less likely to pluck me out of my chair and throw me through the window. After some discussion, Nick and I agreed that it would be best for all concerned if he resigned giving two weeks notice. Hoping that the nervous sweat on my brow was not too noticeable, I shook hands with Nick and wished him well.

I returned to my desk having learned a little lesson. I would never again be tempted to fire someone in a spirit of outraged condemnation. I learned another lesson a few months later when I got a phone call from Nick. He told me that he had a new job and was doing very well. He also said, "I want to thank you for firing me. You know, I never did feel comfortable in that job but I just couldn't bring myself to quit because I didn't know how long it would take me to find another job or whether it would be any better. I'm glad you made the decision for me because it was the best thing that could have happened."

In the years since I have seen many people fired, including myself, and in almost every case the person has found a job better suited to personal abilities and interests. To be fired is not the end of the world. In many cases it is the proper solution for someone who is in the wrong job. It helps no one to keep an employee in a job where, because of lack of interest or aptitude, success is not possible. A person who does not quit that kind of job should be fired for his/her own good. That person will then be forced to find more congenial work, where success and advancement are possible. We do not help people by retaining them in jobs for which they are not fitted. I recently observed an instance in which a salesman was fired after 13 years with a company. During those years he attained his sales target only once. It should have been obvious from the second year on that this man was never going to be a successful salesman. With a great deal of training and persistence he would still never rise above mediocrity. Yet he was kept on, year after year, because he was a nice man with a family, who always seemed to try very hard. As long as company sales continued to grow it was possible to carry a nonproductive salesman, but in 1979 sales fell off and he was fired. The company obviously felt that they were helping the salesman by carrying him through all those unproductive years, but were they? Instead of being forced to find different work at the relatively young age of 33 or 34, the man found himself looking for work at age 45 with a 13-year record of failure.

This does not mean that terminations should be done peremptorily or arbitrarily. Since firing an employee is a serious matter, it should be done in a manner that reflects a company's obligations to its employees and with proper regard for the rights of the terminated employee. Any decision to fire an employee should be based on specific, objective data and not on subjective opinions. There are specific procedures that a manager should follow in firing an unsuitable employee. These procedures were developed to protect the company's interests and the rights of the employee, and to conform with various legal requirements. Every manager should scrupulously follow these procedures.

DISCHARGE FOR CAUSE

In most companies there are four types of actions that are cause for immediate dismissal. An employee fired under one of the causes is usually not entitled to severance pay.

Insubordination

Usually defined as a deliberate and willful refusal to comply with a proper request, or a willful disrespect of authority, or a refusal to work.

Examples:

—Refusal or failure to perform assigned work.

—Failure to comply with established practices.

—Use of profane or abusive language or gestures toward a supervisor.

Before concluding that an employee is insubordinate it is suggested, when appropriate, that you warn the person that his/her action will be deemed insubordinate. You should, if possible, give the individual an opportunity to reconsider before disciplinary action is taken. The reasons for the refusal should be carefully considered as should past performance.

Dishonesty

Usually defined as conduct involving, or tending to involve, money or property, such as theft or misappropriation of money or property. Falsification of records is also considered dishonesty.

Misconduct

Defined as wrong or improper behavior.

Examples:

—Deviation from company policy without proper prior approval.

—Malingering.

—Negligence.

—Gambling.

—Unauthorized solicitations.

—Unauthorized distribution of printed material.

—Fighting on the premises.

—Disorderly or immoral conduct.

—Engaging in illegal activities.

Alcoholism

This customarily involves drinking to the extent that job performance and/or behavior deteriorates, or where efficiency, coordination, relationships, etc. are significantly and adversely affected.

In some companies discharge would be called for only if the condition persists after an employee has declined an opportunity to participate in a rehabilitation program.

In any situation where termination for cause is employed it is the manager's obligation to thoroughly document the misbehavior. Suspicion is not sufficient basis for termination. Specific behavior should be noted and documented with, ideally, witnesses to support the observations of the manager.

DISCHARGE FOR OTHER THAN CAUSE

If it appears that it may be necessary to discharge an employee for reasons other than drunkenness, dishonesty, insubordination, or misconduct, the manager should *give a final warning* before the discharge. The immediate supervisor should clearly spell out to the employee first *orally* and then in *writing* the reason or reasons for the final warning and the corrective action that is required. A definite time limit, not to exceed six months, for proof of improvement should be established and stated in the memo and the employee should be told that lack of sufficient improvement will result in dismissal. The employee's explanation and reaction should be given careful consideration. The purpose of a written final warning is not to set the stage for termination. Its real purpose is to give an employee the opportunity to display that he or she by putting forth a best effort has the capacity to do the job.

A follow-up discussion should take place at the end of the final warning period and the employee's status should be discussed at that time. If the individual shows sufficient improvement to warrant retention, it should be made clear that employment beyond the warning period is contingent upon continued satisfactory work or continued improvement and that no additional warnings within the next six months are required.

All final warning notices should be reviewed with the personnel manager before being communicated to the employee. This will ensure that the final warning policy is being implemented uniformly.

In cases where dismissal subsequently becomes necessary, such action should be taken before the specified warning period elapses. In this event, supervisors should consult with Personnel before informing employees to ensure that the facts warrant dismissal under company policy and employees are aware of their severance pay and other benefits. If no action is taken, or the warning period is not clearly extended, employees may consider that they have sufficiently improved to be retained. Action should not be taken to replace an employee before notice of the impending termination is given to the individual.

While recognizing that firing someone is a distasteful task, the effective manager will not shrink from this duty when necessary. Every effort should be made to match the right person with the right job, but when all efforts have failed and an employee is still nonproductive, the only answer is termination.

18 BUSINESS DRESS

In a listing of qualities that characterize promotable executives, "good appearance" was listed as sixth most important, ahead of such necessary traits as "getting things done with and through people" and "capacity for hard work."[1] How can one's appearance be so important? After all, a manager should be measured on performance rather than appearance, right? Perhaps so, but in business, appearance does affect performance. Much of business consists of working with other people. If cooperative work is to be done effectively, the individuals involved must have trust and confidence in one another. This is true even if the persons have had little contact with one another; mutual trust must be developed immediately. A person's appearance is part of the process by which one person in business says to another, "You can trust me. I know what I am doing. I know what the game of business is all about."

Because, you see, business is a very important game and the superstars are rewarded just as handsomely as the superstars of football or baseball. This book is devoted to the rules of the game and the skills you will need to play the game well. Since we must play the game of business it behooves each of us to play it as skillfully as possible. The rules are important and must be learned. The skills of the game must be acquired, practiced, and used effectively. Finally, the uniform of the game of business should be worn.

In any game, wearing the proper uniform tells the other participants that you know the game and how it is to be played. Wearing a business uniform provides similar assurances. No one would expect to wear a football uniform onto a baseball field and be allowed to compete. Yet, every day one can see young people applying for jobs in business wearing jeans. They are outraged when they are not allowed to play in the game. It is difficult to be sympathetic to people who insist on admittance to a game by demanding that the rules and uniforms be changed.

The business "uniform" developed at the time of the emergence of business in the Industrial Revolution. If the Industrial Revolution had begun and flourished in Japan rather than England, the business uniform would undoubtedly be some type of kimono and business people all over the world would be wearing it, with far more comfort and grace than their present uniform. As it is, Japanese businessmen have had to adopt Western business dress and can share our discomfort. The development of a business uniform served two primary purposes. First, it gave status and identity to people in business. A new social class was rising that did not consist of clergy, nobility, or peasants and business attire was a mark of the new class. Second, it reduced the level of sexuality in business dealings. The old social attire of skin-tight breeches and silk hose for men and low cut gowns for women was inappropriate for the new world of business. The end result is a business uniform designed for men that is as asexual as anything this side of a monk's habit with full hood. It is hot, uncomfortable, and difficult to maintain but it is no worse than hockey or football uniforms. As a manager it is necessary that you know the uniform and wear it properly. It is part of your admission pass into the game and tells people just how serious you are about that game.

The business uniform that will be discussed here applies to all sections of the United States, including southern California. Even there, amid the surfers and the stars and the tax shelters the responsible people of business dress indistinguishably from their counterparts in the east.

The only exceptions to the business dress code are in enterprises that are an outgrowth of the counterculture of the 1960s. I know two substantial businesses in which the accepted uniform is T-shirts, faded jeans, and scuffed boots. One business manufactures imprinted T-shirts, the other is a manufacturer and retailer of health foods. In those businesses jeans and boots comprise the uniform and anyone reporting for work in a vested suit would be regarded with suspicion. In seeking to avoid identification with traditional business and its uniform, those companies have substituted another uniform that must be adhered to just as faithfully. Let us consider the uniform for business starting at the top.

Hats

Men. There are no hats that look good on a young man. If you have a hat give it away. If you grow suitably distinguished with age, at 55 you can buy a pearl gray homburg and wear it with style.

Women. There are some hats that look good on a woman and can be worn with business attire. The most suitable usually are rather plain with a fairly wide brim. Avoid the following:

—Anything resembling a man's hat.

—Anything with fruit or flowers.

—Anything with loud, extreme colors.

—Anything knit.

—Anything with feathers or birds.

—Anything that covers part of the face.

Hairstyle

Men. Short and neat. Any covering of the ears or collar is at your own peril. Moustaches are accepted if neat, not flamboyant, and you are under thirty years of age. Over thirty you are expected to relinquish that last touch of nonconformity. Beards? Forget it. No way, at no age.

Women. Length is not important so long as the face is not obscured. However, the hair should not be so short as to resemble a man's haircut. The hair should give evidence of being cared for. The natural look is best—no teasing or lacquering.

Shirts

Men. Woven, not knit. White, medium to light blue, no other colors. No button-down collars. No starch. Avoid patterns, checks, designs, etc., because it's not worth the trouble trying to find the few that are appropriate. Polyester and cotton blends are best, but get at least 35 percent cotton for appearance. No initials on the pocket or cuff links until you are chairman of the board. If you can wear them, tapered shirts are a great asset. If you can't wear them, diet until you can; I have never known a chief exectuive officer of an American corporation who was more than a few pounds overweight. Never wear a short sleeve shirt. Long sleeves are no more uncomfortable and look immeasurably better.

Women. Much greater variety is possible in colors, patterns, fabrics, etc. Sexiness must be avoided here; blouses should not be too clinging, too open, or too sheer.

Ties

Men. The look you want is quiet, tasteful, expensive. All silk is best. Acetate or polyester is acceptable if very high quality. Look inside the back of the wide end at the lining with diagonal stripes. The number of stripes is an indicator of quality. Do not buy a tie unless it has three or more stripes. Good quality wool ties provide a nice contrast. The colors should be quiet and should match the suit—no brown ties with blue suits, please. Patterns should be small—never, never buy a tie with a large pattern.

Women. No ties, ever. The "butch" look is fatal. A silk scarf is often a pleasing touch.

Suits

Men. Conservative cut, no piping or contrasting stitching. All wool is the only acceptable fabric. It looks better, holds it shape, wears longer, and wrinkles will hang out. It is also reasonably comfortable. If you are in a warm climate, get lightweight wool suits. Do not buy polyester blend suits; they will always look cheap.

Best colors are dark blue, black, dark brown, and dark gray. No light shades of any color. No large checks or patterns. Pinstripes are best, chalk stripes are risky unless you are over six feet tall and have great panache. Glen plaids are acceptable if subdued and of expensive fabric. A black suit should always have a stripe or some type of subdued pattern.

The jacket should fit without pulling across the back or at the waist. Medium lapels, nothing too narrow or too wide. The sleeves should be short enough so that approximately one-quarter inch of the shirt cuff shows.

Trousers should touch the bottom laces of the shoes. Again, not too narrow and no wide flares. Do not use the back pocket for your wallet, it should be carried in the inside pocket of your jacket.

Vests are a welcome note of class. Be careful, the vest must be long enough to cover the belt buckle in front and to touch the belt at the sides so the shirt does not show. Do not wear an open vest, either take it off or keep it buttoned.

Five suits are required for an adequate wardrobe. Wear each suit one day a week. Between wearings, the suits will hang out and pressing will be required only occasionally. Use wooden hangers.

Women. The stipulations for fabric are the same as for men—all wool is best. A much greater variety of colors and designs is acceptable. Again, the aim is a look of subdued elegance.

Unless you are slim and can look elegant in slacks avoid pants suits. Skirts are usually safer and more attractive. Skirt length should be to the bottom of the knee cap or slightly lower. No mid-calf lengths, please. You should be able to cross your legs and have your knees covered. No slit skirts.

Sports Jackets

Men. Not acceptable.

Women. Acceptable if carefully matched to skirt.

Hose

Men. Must be over the calf. Short socks that show bare shanks when you cross your legs are ludicrous. Cotton or wool is best for comfort.

Women. No patterns, designs, or seams. No off colors—the natural look is still the best.

Shoes

Men. No loafers! I don't care who you've seen wearing loafers, they are not part of the business uniform. Wing tips are best. Shoes should be shined but not shiny. Get good shoes and maintain them. Always have full soles put on, half soles are only a little less costly and are harmful to the life and appearance of your shoes. Spend enough to get fully leather lined shoes, they will last longer and be more comfortable. Brown shoes only with brown suits. Black shoes only with blue, gray, or black suits. No exceptions! Belt and shoes should match.

Women. No flats. A heel of some kind is required no matter how tall you are. Good leather is far preferable to any synthetic.

Dresses

Men. Not acceptable, yet.

Women. Unless you have a flawless body avoid knit outfits. A business dress should be almost as subdued in color and design as a man's business suit. Once again the aim is quiet, expensive elegance. Avoid the sexy look; it makes men uncomfortable.

Jewelry

Men. A wedding band. Nothing else! No tie pins, no cuff links, no ID bracelets, no pinky rings, and no gold chains. No class rings—so you graduated from college, big deal! The male of the species, Business Americanus, is unadorned.

Women. One wedding band and everything else in moderation. Jangling bracelets are verboten. All other jewelry should be distinctive without being cheap or flashy.

So there you have it, the proper uniform for the proper business person. It may seem like a great fuss over a minor matter but it is not. The way you dress is important. The people you work with want to know that you are serious about your business and that you have committed yourself to playing the game well. They don't want to look at you in a sport coat and loafers and have to wonder about your commitment to the game. There are enough distractions in business without adding others that are unnecessary. Your appearance should settle, not raise questions about your fitness to play the game.

NOTE

1. Garda W. Bowman, "What Helps or Harms Promotability?" *Harvard Business Review* (January-February 1964).

19 THE REAL SECRET

I s there a secret to success as a manager? Is it knowing the right people or going to the right schools? Some women think it is being plugged into "the old boy network." Others think that hard work and determination are the secrets of success as a manager. Others say there is no secret at all, that the successful manager is one who has a better grasp of the techniques of management.

All these viewpoints are valid in certain cases. However, there really is one thing that is critical to success as a manager. It is a secret that does not seem to be found in any of the literature on management. The sagacious reader might infer the secret, but for some reason it is never explicitly stated. It can more easily be inferred by observing the operations of any company that has enjoyed a measure of success.

A successful company knows where it is going and has people who clearly know what is expected of them. In such a company one will find a management team that understands its market, its customers, and its products. A successful company has managers who set high standards for their people and expect them to be met. A successful company does not operate on the basis of intuition or hunches. It operates on the basis of detailed and reliable information about all aspects of the company and the marketplace. A successful company carefully manages its assets. It has financial controls established so that inventories and receivables are kept within reasonable limits. It requires its managers to obtain authorization for expenditures of any significance.

A successful company plans ahead so that its requirements for capital, supplies, facilities, personnel, and product development are anticipated well in advance. A successful company prepares budgets and forecasts and requires that managers meet their targets in those areas. All the time and effort spent on controls and planning and analysis is aimed toward one goal—predictability. It is from this that the one real secret of management success can be discerned: no surprises!

This principle of predictability is what guides the prudent manager. It is the compass heading by which the manager's career and the work of the department are steered. It provides the framework into which all decisions and actions must fit. Predictability is the impetus behind all budgets, forecasts, operating plans, business plans, strategic plans, computer analysis, and all the other activities that a company engages in to control its own results.

The one overriding aim of managers of American business is to produce a steady, unwavering growth pattern. Depending upon the industry or the company, that growth pattern might be at the rate of 4 percent a year, or 8 percent, or 10 percent, or 15 percent, or even 20 percent. Whatever it is, all the efforts of management are devoted to seeing that the forecasted growth rate is achieved.

Sometimes it can be as disastrous for a company to exceed its sales forecast as it is to fall short of it. Too much success can sometimes be troublesome—witness the plight of the securities industry in the late 1960s. Business was so good that many brokerage firms either went out of business or were forced to merge with other companies to avoid bankruptcy. They couldn't handle the orders they were receiving from their customers. The volume of business was such that many companies strangled to death in their own paperwork. They had not planned for explosive growth.

A large excess of earning in one year is frequently an embarrassment to a company. If nothing else it is an indication that the managers of that company did not really know what was going on. In addition, it raises the expectation among the directors and stockholders that such an increase is to be expected each year. A company whose sales and profits fluctuate widely from one year to another is viewed with suspicion by investors. Such a company has a difficult time borrowing money or raising equity capital. Investors and lending institutions prefer companies that show modest but steady increases in earnings and profits. In short, they prefer predictability.

Wise managers know the value of predictability and make it a motto for themselves and their departments. No surprises! If the officers of a company are not to surprise the directors and stockholders, they must require predictability from their middle and lower managers. Predictability requires that managers fulfill their commitments. Sales targets must be achieved. Expense budgets must not be exceeded. Production quotas must be met. Materials must be available when needed. Shipments must be made on time. Bills must be collected so that operating funds are available. New products must be timed for maximum penetration. All these facets of business activity are interrelated. Anything that affects one area will ultimately affect all other areas.

It is this mutual dependence that makes the work of each manager so critical to the success of a company. The failure of any manager to meet commitments will have a ripple effect that affects work done in many other areas. A modern business is an intricately designed mechanism, which in some ways is delicately balanced. All the parts must mesh together in harmonious and efficient performance. All managers are responsible for the contribution of their groups to the smooth working of the whole.

The successful manager fulfills commitments and never promises more than can be delivered. Brilliance may be needed at times but in the long run dependability is what is valued in a manager. The president of a company loses sleep not because of problems that are known but, rather, the possibility of problems that are still hidden. If the genie of the lamp were to give company presidents one wish, they would opt for a management team that never springs a surprise.

It is impossible to achieve that ideal, but every manager should strive for it. This means that both good and bad news are quickly transmitted up the chain of command. Good news should be passed on only when verified and absolutely certain. Bad news should be transmitted as soon as confirmed. Each manager should consider himself/herself part of an Early Warning System that signals trouble while there is still time to minimize its effect. Do not make the mistake of covering error or hiding problems. Anything of significance is going to surface eventually and the longer it takes, the more serious the consequences for both the manager and the company. The manager's role is to face problems openly, letting superiors know what corrective measures are being taken. One of the most basic rules of business is to make the boss look good. A manager who surprises the boss makes that person look bad. The boss is then faced with the embarrassing situation of having to explain the surprise to a higher manager or, perhaps, a board of directors. Any manager who regularly surprises and embarrasses the boss had better begin to update his/her resume. Any manager who is consistently surprised by subordinates will be found seeking other employment.

"Be neither a surpriser nor a surprisee,
or an ex-employee thou shalt be."

ABOUT THE AUTHOR

James R. Baehler is Manager of Training and Development, CBS Publishing Group. He has held sales and management positions with IBM. He has also been National Sales Manager/Curriculum Materials in the Xerox Education Group; vice-president of marketing for a small educational materials company; and president of Cambosco, Inc., a subsidiary of the Macmillan Company. He has also had several years' experience as an independent management consultant.

Mr. Baehler holds a B.A. from University of Illinois, an M.Sc. from Hobart College, and a certificate from IBM Computer School.